America (USA) Is In A Rebirth, Did The Divine Play A Role

INDIVIDUAL BASIS GOVERNMENT SPENDING IS A FREE MARKET PLACE ECONOMY KILLER.

I did some writing on this subject several years ago and decided to revisit this subject. I'm one that totally believes in having as true a free market place economy as possible. A genuine true free market place economy never fails, that is because it works in line with nature.

Nature has a life and death cycle, which we see as normal, but we know everyone, is going to die sooner or later. What many of us don't seem to know is every economy must have a boom and bust cycle to get rid of negative over-powering anti-survival threats.

Most people believe a bust cycle is a bad thing that should be staved off forever. The reason a true free market place economy is so successful and never fails is because of its not so obvious discipline.

A true free market place economy with it's purging power discipline protects itself and prevents other threats in a society from growing out of control. "Free and Natural" are two key words that maintain a healthy true free market place economy.

In my view there are only two players in an economy no matter how complicated it may seem, those two players are a seller (merchant) and a buyer (consumer). And if government would just stay with collecting taxes and act as a neutral referee a free market place economy would police and manage itself far better than what's happening now.

America (USA) Is In A Rebirth, Did The Divine Play A Role

If government had butted out our society would have a strong nuclear and extended family system, proper norms and traditions would be instilled and enforced in our very young, and very few people would be dependent on government for their sole survival.

So, when a bust cycle did show up to purge out anti-survival threats like culture rot and moral decay it would be a little more than "A piece of cake". Today our super provider welfare state government is dumping billions upon billions into our private economy claiming to help the poor and needy.

But, look what that has got us twenty trillion in debt and the destruction of our culture and morals. Plus, we are left with no emergency backup capacity to barter and trade if our economy collapses. I don't know what kind of economy we have today, but it is not even close to a true free market place economy, period.

In my view the only way for government to aid and help the poor and needy without destruction to the national economy is to use a dual track system. In my view only two things that can save the USA and Western civilization, get rid of all minimum wage laws entirely and stop giving out billions upon billions of government dollars on an individual basis to be dumped into our private national economies.

What I mean by dual track is use a separate system to keep all individual basis government money from being dumped into our private free

America (USA) Is In A Rebirth, Did The Divine Play A Role

market place economy, thereby distorting it and driving up the cost of living.

I'm one that believes that helping the poor and needy should first be done by the family, extended family, church, community organizations, and government last and then on a set temporary basis only. Otherwise, government dependency will destroy the nuclear family by taking away the survival need for it to exist.

All of that said: Government must come to the aid and help the poor and needy, period. But, the only way the government can help the poor and needy without destroying our private free market place economy is to use a dual track system.

Dual track: Government must establish or contract out its own commissaries, clinics, and housing units and use separate tokens or script as the currency for all that qualify, that will prevent mass government dumping of money into our private national economy.

The amount of government spending doesn't matter, it is the individual basis spending dumped into our private U.S. economy that contaminates and drives up the cost of living for all of us. Also, a minimum wage law binds the purging power of a free market place economy and won't let it protect itself or the nations culture, morals, and values.
SIRMANS LOG: 21 DECEMBER 2016, 1650 HOURS.

SO CALLED "FAKE NEWS" IS BULL S...
Sure, I believe the November 2016 presidential election was a dilemma between two extremes.

America (USA) Is In A Rebirth, Did The Divine Play A Role

Also, I believe if the liberals had won it would have been the end of individual freedom in America (USA). I wrote at the beginning of the primary that I believed that Mr. Trump was a catalyst to a main event, to what we'll just have to wait and see.

I don't know who coined the phrase "Fake news"; but I feel it had to be a liberal. The words themselves are a contradiction, news is news, it can be true, untrue, good, bad, or ugly it's still real, not fake. This is just another way the shallow minded liberals distort reality. Besides: there is already a word for factually untrue news, it is called propaganda.

For many years liberals has almost totally dominated the news in the USA, but today that is no longer the case. With the Internet and talk radio most people today of sound mind and common sense no longer fall prey to liberal hogwash and propaganda.

I'm one that is beginning to feel the U.S. may have a chance of being saved from total liberalism self-destruction. Thank God. Still, in my view only repealing our insane arch-evil 1938 socialist minimum wage law can save us.

That will untie and give us back a genuine true free market place economy with the purging power discipline to restore the USA culturally, morally, and financially back to greatness. (Click here to understand slave blood killings)
SIRMANS LOG: 16 DECEMBER 2016, 1305 HOURS.

RAW CRUDE ECONOMIC SURVIVAL IN THIS GREAT WRITER'S VIEW

America (USA) Is In A Rebirth, Did The Divine Play A Role

To whom this may concern: Here is some very good sound advice, forget about trying to solve problems like getting rid of Obama care, bringing jobs back, and countless other insurmountable problems. Instead, to the very wise the solution is very simple, concentrate on repealing our insane arch-evil 1938 socialist minimum wage law.

If that is repealed then a genuine true free market place economy itself will do everything you are trying and more, including booming the economy and bringing back jobs. Otherwise, the powers that be will continue chasing falling stars at the end of a rainbow, and end up just another casualty of our all powerful welfare state, duh. And the liberals will continue their march to our total self-destruction.
SIRMANS LOG: 11 DECEMBER 2016, 1201 HOURS.

HAIL TO THE CHIEF! TRUMP THE SAVIOR!
As a writer I consider myself to be a wise realist, but quite often I'm wrong. My take on Presidential elect Trump bringing jobs back and keeping jobs in America is like putting a finger in a dike. With a 100 pound liberal induced welfare state millstone around our neck we can barely compete let along win an economic race.

I have said it a thousand times the evil 1938 socialist minimum wage law killed the purging and self-disciplining power in our USA economy. What we have left today is a phony weak p.... of an economy that has allowed the almost total destruction of our culture and moral values.

I believe the sole purpose for the November 2016 republican Trifecta wins was to save the U.S. Supreme Court and repeal our 1938 minimum wage law; anything else is wishful thinking and a

America (USA) Is In A Rebirth, Did The Divine Play A Role

pipe dream in my view. The republicans think they can manage and save our welfare state. It ain't gonna happen is my take on the matter.

I'm not speaking in jest on this matter folks, our welfare state is just simply too powerful and well established to be defeated or taken down to size, period. Nothing on earth can seriously reform or take down to size our USA welfare state, except repealing our insane arch-evil 1938 socialist minimum wage law. And I'll bet the farm on that.

In the long run it is simply impossible to support a welfare state financial burden and have a military capable of defending the nation. Not to speak of the upkeep and maintenance of our infrastructure. Repealing our 1938 minimum wage law will slowly wean the USA out of our crippling welfare state financial burden before the cost finally suck the nation dry.

SIRMANS LOG: 04 DECEMBER 2016, 1211 HOURS.

COLD REALITY AND THE GOSPEL TRUTH:
As a writer I write it as I see it, I can't make anyone believe or agree with anything I write. In my view only two things can save the USA from total destruction due to out of control liberalism. First and top priority is our evil 1938 socialist minimum wage law; it must be repealed for the USA to have any chance for long-term survival.

The second thing is we must return to a currency that has its value in the currency itself. And that means coins made up of gold, silver, copper, or other precious metals, period. The core problem and threat to the USA is it is morally and culturally bankrupted.

America (USA) Is In A Rebirth, Did The Divine Play A Role

Only instilling in our very young proper norms and traditions within a strong nuclear and extended family system can save the USA long-term. And no amount of more phony money can bring about the discipline to make that happen. Real survival discipline today is a sick joke due to our welfare state and out of control liberalism. God save my beloved USA, I ask in your name. Thank you in advance.

VOTER RECOUNT COMMENT, (Not to be taken seriously).
Anytime liberals start recounting votes this writer get nervous. If the Supreme Court hadn't stopped them they would still be recounting the Bush VS Gore ballots. Almost everyone knows if an election is close the liberals almost always can find an overlooked misplaced box of ballots with 20,000 or more 90 percent in their favor. Duh.
SIRMANS LOG: 27 NOVEMBER 2016, 2317 HOURS.

COMING TRADE WAR:
OK, the USA being an entrenched welfare state really means politically in practice it is almost impossible for the republicans to reform it, or save it from liberalism final destruction.

However, reforming and saving the USA would be a piece of cake to a genuine true free market place economy. Regretfully, our corrupt p.... of an economy is tied and bounded by a 1938 minimum wage law that kills its purging and disciplining power; otherwise a true free market place economy would do the reforming the republicans want and keep them in office blame free.

Due to out of control liberalism there is no doubt in

America (USA) Is In A Rebirth, Did The Divine Play A Role

this writer's mind that culture rot and moral decay has deteriorated to snake belly level in the USA. Very soon the American people will be demanding an authoritarian ruled government just for the sake of order. The Trump election was just the tip of the iceberg.

Trade war:
The only way the USA can survive our coming trade war is to first repeal the 1938 minimum wage law. If not, the cost burden of our liberal induced welfare state will almost instantly collapse our economy, which will cause mass civil disorder and mass starvation, trust me.

Another thing, the biggest mistake the republicans can make is to forget we live in a well-established welfare state. And liberals and liberalism still dominates damn near everything in it. To some degree almost the whole nation is dependent minded, spoiled, and pampered. And the first sign of any real pain due to cuts in social programs republicans will get the boot.

Only repealing the 1938 minimum wage law can set the USA economy free to save our freedom, but the republicans will never do that, what a shame.
SIRMANS LOG: 19 NOVEMBER 2016, 1743 HOURS.

EACH PRIVATE BUSINESS MUST BE FREE TO SET ITS OWN PRICES AND WAGES, NOT THE FEDERAL GOVERNMENT.
With the Trifecta win the insane arch-evil 1938 socialist federal minimum wage law can now be repealed. Once the minimum wage law is repealed and gotten rid of entirely, sure wages will slowly drop but the cost of living will drop twice as much, which is a great advantage.

America (USA) Is In A Rebirth, Did The Divine Play A Role

Let the states and cities set their own minimum wage laws if they choose. But, it castrates and blocks the discipline power of a true free market place economy when set on a large-scale nation wide by the federal government.

The problem with the USA economy is too much government involvement, let each business set its own prices and wages and the economy will police and manage itself. Otherwise, there are just too many variables to truly and safely predict anything.

Believe it or not until each private American business is free to set its own prices and wages it is impossible to prevent a total USA economic collapse, period. I'm one that believes there was a divine element in the surprised Trifecta win. The liberal enacted insane arch-evil 1938 socialist federal minimum wage law may now be in the cross hairs. And I'm doing a happy dance.

Repealing our 1938 federal minimum wage law will solve the nations health care problem by lowering our cost of living to where the people can pay their own health care cost out of pocket. The fact is we are a broke nation already 20 trillion deep in debt, we simply will not survive unless we break the federal governments strangle hold on the neck of our economy by repealing the federal minimum wage law, period.

The USA economy is a private institution, sure the government can tax it but it doesn't own the economy. Until the "New Deal" liberal programs in the 1930's injected socialism into the economy every private business had always had the power to set its own prices and wages.

America (USA) Is In A Rebirth, Did The Divine Play A Role

Now, look what we got, chaos and $20,000,000,000,000 in debt. Plus, the USA government has cruelly irresponsibly made millions upon millions solely dependent on government for their only survival. What is going to happen to all of these people when this government can no longer borrow enough to meet it obligations?

Every healthy free market place economy is going to have a boom and bust cycle the same as our survival has a life and death cycle. How else can nature get rid of overpowering moral decay, culture rot, and other anti-survival negativity without a bust cycle?

For over six thousand years with strong nuclear and extended family systems civilization survived through economic bust cycles, but that is almost impossible when our U.S. nuclear and extended family system is in almost total ruins.

I am all about survival and saving lives. I don't want to see millions upon millions of lives needlessly lost due to the destruction of our nuclear and extended family system, which I link directly to our insane arch-evil 1938 socialist federal minimum wage law. Repealing the 1938 minimum wage law and rebuilding a strong nuclear and extending family system is the only hope of the USA surviving, period.

Sure, advocating for repealing the federal minimum wage law is butting my head up against a brick wall because there has never been a case of a country changing course even knowing it is headed toward sure doom. But, I feel "To try and keep trying is the greatest of all virtues".
SIRMANS LOG: 09 NOVEMBER 2016, 2250 HOURS.

America (USA) Is In A Rebirth, Did The Divine Play A Role

THE CURSE OF THE U.S. LIBERAL NEWS MEDIA:
This writer feels the bias corrupt liberal news media believed that the easiest way to keep a liberal in the White House was they could easily steamroll over Trump. Otherwise, today Trump may not even be in the picture in this writer's view. This whole debacle can be placed at the feet of the shallow minded know it all liberal news media.

LIBERALISM CRAP:
Crime, crime, crime, for God sake people! The basic human personality is shaped by the age of six. And if a society can't crime proof its young by the age of ten it probably never will. Give me a break people! You solve behavior problems by instilling in the very young proper norms, traditions, and moral values, period. What else can one with an ounce of wisdom expect when our nuclear and extended family system is shot all to hell.

This is an article I should not be writing, and especially right before an election. But, I feel I must before I change my mind. I believe the USA and the entire survival of western civilization may be at stake.

NOTE: If the liberals gain control over our U.S. Supreme Court and finish killing off our dying country, all credit goes to our bias corrupt liberal news media. In this writer's view they are shallow and stupid with weak survival instincts. Yet, feel they know best and have all of the answers.

For several years now I have kept up a constant drumbeat to repeal or get rid of all government enforced minimum wage laws, period. I feel all

America (USA) Is In A Rebirth, Did The Divine Play A Role

wage gains should be gotten by means of unions or private means only because government enforced minimum wage laws castrates a true free market place economy.

I believe I have the perspective and raw wisdom to dissect the inner workings of an economy as well as anyone. And I have concluded that free floating prices and wages makes up the lifeblood of a true free market place economy. I also feel that an economy just like life itself should have a healthy rebirth cycle, and nothing does that better than a true free market place economy.

For civilization to exist it must have some type of economic system to function on, but economics is not the foundation for human survival and existence. The nuclear and extended family system is the foundation for human survival, period. And why it is a must for human survival is it instills in the very young proper norms, traditions, and moral values.

Plus, there has never been a civilization or society that survived without a strong nuclear and extended family system, period. "The process of natural selection" is a supreme law of nature. But, the key to understanding this law is it is based on "Need". For anything to exist in nature it must have a survival need, otherwise it slowly starts ceasing to exist. Fish living in pitch-dark caves doesn't have eyes, they don't have a survival need for eyes.

So, when the welfare state rudely took over the nuclear and extended family system as the "Great white father" provider that took away the "Need" for the traditional family provider. Once government took over the traditional family

America (USA) Is In A Rebirth, Did The Divine Play A Role

provider role no one enforced and carried out instilling in the very young proper norms, traditions, and moral values anymore. That is why the African American race is rudderless and killing each other off like mad dogs.

Civilization existed with trade and bartering long before a currency (money) was invented. In fact some American Indian populations was very large, though I don't think the American Indians ever-used money as a currency. Sure, money and the economy are extremely important, but civilization cannot exist for very long without a strong nuclear and extended family system already in place, period.

Through ignorance liberalism has almost totally destroyed the USA nuclear and extended family system by eliminating a survival need for it. Now, when our weak Phony economy finally collapses no strong nuclear and extended family foundation will exist to rebuild upon. Duh. That may drive modern civilization all the way back to the Stone Age, period. Think about it.

Again, the thing about a minimum wage law is: It robs a free market place economy of its power to protect the nation's culture, morals, and spiritual values. A minimum wage law won't allow our economy to protect itself and the nation by keeping inflation purged out.

An inflated currency is a Godsend to liberals because without an inflated currency they wouldn't have the funds to buy votes and power. Way back the liberals corrupted the system by giving out tax funded freebies to grab and keep them in power, which shows how shallow they are because nothing in life is free someone always pays. Yet, giving out

America (USA) Is In A Rebirth, Did The Divine Play A Role

tax funded freebies kept liberals in total control of the U.S. House of Representatives for 40 consecutive years, that is where our "Expect something for nothing" mentality comes from.

Liberals and Liberalism is not a bad thing in fact it is the spice of life when kept under control, but as a rule they are shallow and can be dangerous when in power. Right now in the USA and Western Europe liberalism is totally out of control. And the only thing that can counter balance and stop them from bringing on our total self-destruction, is to repeal and ban all government enforced minimum wage laws, period. Nothing else can stop them. (Click here to understand slave blood killings)

A FUTURE GLIMPSE OF A LIBERAL CONTROLLED U.S. SUPREME COURT
Folks, as a writer let me give you a brief glimpse of the USA if liberals get total control of the U.S. Supreme Court. Lets just say it is now a little after 12:00 noon the 20th day of January 2017, Liberals now have the power to rule the U.S. supreme Court and will have the last and final say on what the law is.

The African Americans, the women, and the masses of government dependents that gave the liberals this awesome power will rue the day. Free speech and freedom of the press will be the first casualties. The legislative branch will become mostly ceremonial.

Being in total control of the U.S. Supreme Court a liberal president may resort to presidential executive orders and a Supreme Court backup to rule. A liberal controlled Supreme Court may

America (USA) Is In A Rebirth, Did The Divine Play A Role

rubber-stamp almost every do-good liberal presidential executive order that comes along, period.

The poor will no longer be pampered they will be forced to pay and do their share because the first ten amendments known as the bill of rights will no longer be worth the paper it is printed on. Mass civil unrest and order will quickly get out of hand and private ownership of guns will be banned as the final solution.

I believe Liberals actually see the people like cogs in a giant machine not as individuals with feelings and rights. True conservatives are restrained by an internal moral code, but you get between a liberal lion/lioness and power, then your ass may be grass. I will close by saying; if you think things are upside down now which is due to liberalism, you haven't seen anything yet.

Liberals already control education, the news media, and damn near everything else in this country. And to give them absolute power over the U.S. Supreme Court with the last and final say on what the law is, that's sheer madness, period.
SIRMANS LOG: 14 OCTOBER 2016, 1026 HOURS.

THE POWER OF ENLIGHTENMENT
The things I used to do I don't do anymore. That is what can happen when someone has seen the light and become enlightened. Corrupt liberalism is putting the nation down into a slimy gutter; how can you expect anyone to come out smelling like a rose, period.

Speaking only for himself this writer says to

America (USA) Is In A Rebirth, Did The Divine Play A Role

kowtow, knuckle under, chicken out, punk out, suck up, roll over, grab both ankles, or just plain submit and give in to our 24-7 corrupt discriminating liberal news media propaganda machine; never, never, never... "No guts no glory".

The nation is beginning to drown in a liberal sea of muck and slime, and that will be the nation's future if liberalism gain complete control of the U.S. Supreme Court on November the 8th and have the last and final say on everything. The nation's survival is on the line, not how much dirt is in someone's distance past, some people and circumstances do change.

"The road to hell is paved with good intentions, wanting something for nothing, weakness, ignorance, and trusting in government instead of the people are all absent of true virtue". There is at least a fifty fifty chance on November 8th ignorance and trusting in government over the people will win the day, if that happens Mr. Trump won't lose, the nation will.

SIRMANS LOG: 07 OCTOBER 2016, 2127 HOURS.

WHY INDIVIDUAL FREEDOM IS SO RARE IN HISTORY?
The reason why individual freedom is so rare and hard to keep is because of liberals and liberalism. The "Iron fist" has been the norm throughout history to govern and rule people because it is natural for people to become liberal and take the course of least resistance in life. But, there is very little lasting enjoyment and order in anything without a balance of conservatism as discipline.

It may not seem so, but there is no greater disciplinarian than a genuine true free market place

America (USA) Is In A Rebirth, Did The Divine Play A Role

economy. Unrestricted it will purge out waste, disorder, greed, or anything threatening. However, any kind of wage control blockage stops its natural freedom to reward or purge which is its disciplining power.

The 1938 minimum wage law killed the discipline power in the USA free market place economy. That is why moral decay and culture rot is out of control and unless the 1938 minimum wage law is repealed authoritarian rule will be forced upon us soon, we must have order.

SIRMANS LOG: 04 OCTOBER 2016, 1436 HOURS.

CONCERNING THE FLINT WATER CRISIS:
Liberalism for all practical purpose has made the USA almost ungovernable in this writer's view. Far too many Americans believe the USA can keep borrowing and spending money it doesn't have forever, which is a ball-faced lie. What is going to happen when no other country has the ability to give us a loan, duh.

All "Government Money" or income originates from some form of private business profit, period. Yet, no one else besides me tries to educate the public of this basic economic fact. Business profit is the golden egg, yet liberals and liberalism is killing the goose that lays the golden egg by regulating and taxing it to death. No private business profit means no government income, period.

The only things government can support and survive long term are the military, the interior, and the very few things the people can't do for themselves. And the thing government should never do is become a social and family provider other than on a set temporary basis, it leads to

America (USA) Is In A Rebirth, Did The Divine Play A Role

total destruction. Or course, rational deep thinking of this sort tends to be beyond most shallow minded liberals.

Never in history has the poor ever been liberal and corrupted, yet, our liberal enacted welfare state has made them and nearly half the nation die hard liberals. Today there is simply far too many people feeding at the government trough. Government in the social and family provider business is like feeding on yourself by eating your seed corn or drinking your priming water.

The people must get back to depending on themselves like before the "New Deal" because our phony weak p.... of an economy is definite going to soon totally collapse. And the only way the people can get back to depending on themselves is for our insane arch-evil 1938 socialist minimum wage law to be repealed, period.

Sure, there will be much hardship, but that is the only way the USA is going to survive intact as a free nation, period. Otherwise, liberalism will continue its march to our total self-destruction by totally collapsing our economy. Already, it may be too late to keep the USA from splitting into bits and pieces from the coming collapse.

SIRMANS LOG: 28 SEPTEMBER 2016, 1001 HOURS.

THE #1 THREAT TO USA IS NOT WHAT EVERYONE THINKS?

In this writers view it is irresponsible and national suicide to give liberals total control of the USA Supreme Court and final say on everything; there can be no recovery from this. Mass civil unrest will become inevitable and quickly demand some form of authoritarian rule just to maintain order.

America (USA) Is In A Rebirth, Did The Divine Play A Role

Without a doubt the nation's sheer survival is on the line and at stake, period. The time for feel good talk is over; the rocky road ahead is in the hands of the voters. Sure, it is a dilemma, but there may not be a second chance.
SIRMANS LOG: 24 SEPTEMBER 2016, 0914 HOURS.

UPDATE:
Writer's personal view on "Mr. Trump" is he actually is a liberal that finally saw the light and has been enlightened. A genuine true conservative may be constrained by morals and other factors whereas with liberals it is a horse of a different color. Sometimes it takes fire to fight fire.

In fact there is nothing innate about being liberal, they are the most changeable of all ideologues. Many liberals have become conservative overnight after being slammed upside the head by a mugger or robbed of their possessions. "Lack of survival awareness" is the liberals Achilles heel in this writer's view.

Lets just say Mr. Trump wins, his main advantage is I believe he will save the U.S. Supreme Court from a complete liberal take over. Other than that I don't believe anything or anyone can prevent a complete global economic collapse, period. But, in my view that is not the main point, the main point is a healthy society should always be able to survive and live through any boom or bust cycle, regardless.

However, that can only be done with a strong nuclear and extended family system in place along with a fair amount of emergency bartering capacity with small farmers and home gardeners. But, the

America (USA) Is In A Rebirth, Did The Divine Play A Role

liberals have destroyed all of that in the USA by enacting our insane arch-evil 1938 socialist minimum wage law.

A minimum wage law destroys the discipline power of a free market place economy, which allows inflation and liberalism to grow unchecked out of control and will eventually destroy everything.
SIRMANS LOG: 16 SEPTEMBER 2016, 0048 HOURS.

UPDATE:
As a great writer to all of the great genius's out there here is my take on the 2016 presidential election: Liberalism has never had total control of the U.S. Supreme Court, but if the liberals win the presidency in 2016 for the first time they will get total control of the U.S. Supreme Court and have the final say on everything.

I may be a lot of things but the village idiot is not one of them. I blame liberalism for the almost total destruction of western civilization itself. Trumpism is something we can recover from and fight another day, but there can be no recovery if the liberals get total control over the U.S. Supreme Court and our survival.

One can't protect or defend what one is not aware of, which is the fatal flaw of liberalism. A strong survival instinct can only be derived from some form of real life hardship or struggle, it has to be physical experienced. Right now the USA is spending itself out of existence but liberals are unaware of any problem with that and wants to spend even more reckless.

Folks, if liberals get total control over the survival of the USA we are done, cooked. They will first

America (USA) Is In A Rebirth, Did The Divine Play A Role

take our guns, and then mass civil unrest will rule the day, which will make some form of authoritarian rule inevitable. Sure, I am wrong on a lot of things I write about but liberal chaos is not one of them, without discipline there is no lasting enjoyment of anything in life. And lack of discipline is one of the biggest flaws of all with liberalism, period.
SIRMANS LOG: 13 SEPTEMBER 2016, 1119 HOURS.

I'm one that truly believes that out of control liberalism is by far the greatest threat to the survival of the USA and Western Europe. You can call me crazy, a nut case, or whatever but that is the way I see it.

I can't see the USA and Western Europe ever getting rid of their minimum wage laws, but that is the only thing that can provide the discipline to get liberalism back under control, period. I am one of the very few with the depth and perspective to dissect an economy and isolate this obvious fact, period.
SIRMANS LOG: 07 SEPTEMBER 2016, 2159 HOURS

ECONOMICS: THIS THING THEY CALL GROWTH IS A FALLACY
Beginning with the minimum wage law in 1938 using the term growth is one of the biggest lies in economics that have ever been told. Sure, in a true free market place economy like before the 1938 minimum wage law the term growth meant real true growth.

That is simply because it is impossible to have consumer inflation and a welfare state absent a

America (USA) Is In A Rebirth, Did The Divine Play A Role
minimum wage law. But, after the liberals enacted the 1938 minimum wage law what is now called growth is some kind of a phony blend of mostly inflation with hardly any real growth to speak of. And it's been that way ever since 1938. Today it takes $50.00 or more to buy what $5.00 would eighty years ago.

Ain't no sense of me rambling on and on, I'll just get to the point one way or another our insane arch-evil 1938 socialist minimum wage law must go. If we don't do it ourselves soon mother natures supreme law of "Natural Selection" is going to do it for us. And that means totally collapsing the economy, period.

I have been yelling out a primal survival stress call for many years now, what else is there to be done? Untold millions are going to starve to death. We have very little foundation like a strong nuclear and extended family system and an adequate supply of small farmers and home gardeners for emergency bartering capacity left to rebuild upon.

A total USA economy collapse may set modern civilization back to the Stone Age, for real.
SIRMANS LOG: 28 AUGUST 2016, 2209 HOURS.

OUR WELFARE ANNIVERSARY
Because of its twenty-year anniversary I see the welfare debate is being tossed around. The blessing I have is I have the perspective and depth to see pass fog and bull and bore right to the heart of most problems. The first thing is if you don't understand human survival everything you say is empty rhetoric anyway.

America (USA) Is In A Rebirth, Did The Divine Play A Role

Anyone that has any knowledge of history should know that across all cultures one thing has been a constant for human survival for over six thousand years. This thing has proven itself to sustained life and has withstood the test of time. If you don't know what I'm talking about by now you don't have a true sense of history or what it takes for human survival, period.

This thing I'm talking about is the "Nuclear and extended family system". There has never been a society in the history of mankind across all cultures that survived without a strong "Nuclear and extended family system" in place, period. Yet, the USA and Western Europe with their welfare states has left the traditional strong "Nuclear and extended family system" in almost total ruins.

With that being the case hardly anyone is making sure proper norms and traditions is instilled in the very young. In far too many cases a strong male disciplinarian head of household is nowhere to be found. And even if a male is in the picture he is there for stud service at her whim.

It is a waste of time talking about reforming welfare because it is just one more monster in our liberalism swamp. I can see right to the core of our welfare problem, and tell you the way to solve it. The best way is to kill two birds with one stone by starving the beast and draining the swamp. It is very simple; just repeal the arch-evil 1938 socialist minimum wage law, period.

That act would starve the liberalism beast to death and drain the liberalism swamp all at the same time. If that happened it would also untie the USA economy and give it back its disciplining power and bring on a booming economy all at the same time.

America (USA) Is In A Rebirth, Did The Divine Play A Role

Otherwise, it will be impossible for the USA economy not to totally collapse soon.

Don't take my word, any USA economist in private will tell you the same thing if he/she trust you.
SIRMANS LOG: 21 AUGUST 2016, 1332 HOURS.

USA ECONOMICALLY INSANE ARCH-EVIL 1938 SOCIALIST MINIMUM WAGE LAW:
Enough is enough, if congress is not going to repeal this evil 1938 law, me or someone must contest this evil law in court to the highest level, period. The 10th amendment is there for a reason; each state should have the power to set its own minimum wage law or if to set one at all.

A minimum wage law gives the government total power over all property rights, all production rights, and all distribution rights. There is no greater governmental power on earth than to have a minimum wage law. Plus, it turns a free market place into a p.... economy with no power to discipline itself or to protect the country's culture and morals.

It is impossible to save the USA unless our evil 1938 minimum wage law is repealed. Only a genuine true free market place economy can save the USA from the liberals and total doom, period. And that can never happen with a minimum wage law in place.
SIRMANS LOG: 19 AUGUST 2016, 1129 HOURS.

AUTHORITARIAN RULE IS INEVITABLE IF THE LIBERALS WIN THE NOVEMBER 2016

America (USA) Is In A Rebirth, Did The Divine Play A Role

PRESIDENTIAL ELECTION
One thing I have learned is individual freedom cannot exist very long without a non minimum wage genuine true free market place economy in place to maintain societal discipline, period. I hate to admit it but I believe after our November 2016 presidential election individual freedom in the USA will be lost forever.

If the liberals win they will take over the U.S. Supreme Court. If that happens there will be no saving individual freedom, liberalism will have the final say on everything. It shouldn't take a rocket scientist to know that mass civil unrest will only be a matter of time and then authoritarian rule will become inevitable. God save the USA.

NOTE CONCERNING TRUMP:
The way this writer see it is when you have a corrupt anti-survival hostile liberal news media hell bent on destroying you: Damn the torpedoes! Full speed ahead!

An aggressive, persistent, and determine person can never be counted out; unforeseen forces tends to come to the aid of someone like that.

The last three republican presidential losers let the anti-survival corrupt liberal news media steam roll over them without even breaking a sweat. Not so with Trump, at least he will take them to the mat.
SIRMANS LOG: 13 AUGUST 2016, 0917 HOURS.

GREAT WRITER, FREDDIE LEE SIRMANS, SR. SHARES HIS STRUGGLES
Sure; I'm neurotic and not normal and never will be. But, one thing I'm not and never will be is a

America (USA) Is In A Rebirth, Did The Divine Play A Role

loser. All of my life I have been counted out and sometimes ridiculed, laughed at, and told as a very young child that I would never amount to anything. Yet, today as a seventy three year old I am still plodding along like a zombie trying in my own way to do good and make this a better world.

I'm not educated, I have never took a computer course in my life and have never read Adam Smith or any of the great economic thinkers. But, I understand and can dissect an economy as well as anyone. So, when I tell you our insane Arch-evil 1938 socialist minimum wage law must be repealed to save the USA and western civilization, You had better believe it, period.
SIRMANS LOG: 19 JULY 2016, 2256 HOURS.

COP KILLING GALORE! OMG!
Liberalism gone amuck is why our societal discipline has gone to hell in the USA. Only a genuine true free market place economy has the discipline and power to save the USA and western civilization from total self-destruction.

The only workable solution is obvious, the insane arch-evil 1938 socialist minimum wages law must be repealed to free and untie our USA economy before it is too late. Without a doubt I am right on this even if this supernatural wisdom is never heeded. Glory be to God.
SIRMANS LOG: 17 JULY 2016, 2257 HOURS.

RELIGION TURNOUT WILL DECIDE NOVEMBER 2016 PRESIDENTIAL ELECTION
The religious people are all in and totally committed to pushing back on all of this mass culture rot and moral decay that is taking down

America (USA) Is In A Rebirth, Did The Divine Play A Role

this great land of the free and home of the brave.

They know this is the last chance to save the USA from mass same sex marriages, the morning after pill, and mass killing on demand in the womb. Even an idiot should know that our future survival as a nation is in grave danger.

The religious people they all will be turning out in droves in November 2016 to put a stop to this insane madness that is determined to make us all amoral misfits. However, today most low-income voters don't give a damn about good morals unless it pleases their own personal biases.

We all should be praying for our future because a totally economic collapse is going to soon hit causing millions upon millions to starve to death. Of course I pray something like this will never happen, but anyone that thinks it can't ever happen is a fool.

Our nuclear and extended family system is in almost total ruins. Plus, with our mass culture rot and moral decay we now have practically no foundation left to rebuild upon, period. When I yell, scream, jump up and down, and even cry to repeal our insane arch-evil 1938 socialist minimum wage law that is a primal last chance stress call for the survival of my beloved homeland. Glory be to God.

When will men/women of common sense and sound judgment finally realize that the days of a welfare state is over, I guess circumstance will just have to show them the hard way.

SIRMANS LOG: 12 JULY 2016, 1120 HOURS.
PS: I believe it will be a lot less likely that Trump will get impeached if Newt is selected for vice president??? The liberal lawmakers are already 100

America (USA) Is In A Rebirth, Did The Divine Play A Role

percent for it, and then sprinkle in a few republicans and it will be done.

GREAT MANDATORY MUST READ ARTICLES BY WRITER FREDDIE L SIRMANS SR.
In this writers view it is irresponsible and national suicide to give liberals total control of the USA Supreme Court and final say on what the law is; there can be no recovery. Mass civil unrest getting out of hand is inevitable and will quickly demand some form of authoritarian rule just to maintain order.

A liberal controlled Supreme Court will backup a presidential executive order banning private ownership of all hand guns without a doubt, period. And it will be only be a matter of time before they come after the long guns people have in their homes.

Without a doubt the nation's sheer survival is on the line and at stake, period. The time for feel good talk is over; the rocky road ahead is in the hands of the voters. Sure, it is a dilemma, but there may not be a second chance to save this last great bastion of true individual freedom left in the world today.
SIRMANS LOG: 24 SEPTEMBER 2016, 0914 HOURS.

RACISM: SO, WHAT ABOUT IT?
Writer's personal view on "Mr. Trump" is he actually is a liberal that finally saw the light and has been enlightened.

There are some subjects I tend to avoid and stay away from and "Racism" is one of them. I'm not good at pulling punches and I believe in calling a

America (USA) Is In A Rebirth, Did The Divine Play A Role

spade a spade, period. I view character and showing respect far more important than whether one may or may not be a racist, besides who really knows what someone is hiding deep down in his/her heart anyway. Someone laughing in your face may be the biggest racist of all.

If one has a secure and independent mindset who gives a damn what someone else may or may not think as long as they can't hurt you. As long as there are different races racism is going to exist in some form to some degree, period. The real problem and threat as far as I'm concern is bigotry when race is used to punish or hurt another race.

I think the real problem with my race, which is the African American race, is we have not shedded our dependency slave mentality. Sure, it kept us alive during and right after slavery in a totally hostile environment, but now we are responsible for our own survival as a race and as individuals. We act like the white man the government or someone else is responsible for our personal survival.

From a mentality point of view I think we view other blacks like inferior competing siblings instead of independent adults that need to help and support each other. In my view that is the reason behind all of this mass senseless violence in black communities.

If the young Negro child has never been conditioned to show self-restraint, self-responsibility, and self-accountability then he won't have a strong conscience to guide and protect him for the rest of his life. The welfare state and liberalism is to blame for this sad state, and now for the most part the Negro male has lost his instinct for male dominance, even in slavery he

America (USA) Is In A Rebirth, Did The Divine Play A Role

never lost that.

We don't see other African Americans as lovable and needed racial family members like before the "New Deal". But, instead see an inferior rival threat undeserving of respect. Boom. Before the "New Deal" blacks were forced to need and support each other, and black culture and enterprise thrived far, far more than today.

Also, blacks were beginning to shed its dependency slave mentality and bam; the "New Deal" booted the black male disciplinarian out of the house. I've said enough and will close by saying this: As long as our welfare state last African Americans will be voting 90 percent plus Democrat until dooms day, it is because of an unneeded imaginary crutch in my view.

SIRMANS LOG: 25 AUGUST 2016, 2151 HOURS.

RAW! CRUDE! MIND BOGGLING! THE REAL TRUTH ABOUT THE BLACK PSYCHE IN AMERICA

The betterment of a race or people must be pulled up from the top by its elites because only they have the resources. But, because of Du Bois's victory over the minds of black Americans the black elites has left black communities in almost total ruins in my view.

I believe only blacks can save their own communities, no other race or people is going to do it, period. At the time many decades ago Booker T lost the battle for the minds of black people to Du Bois. Well, I'm one that believes that Booker T may have lost the battle but he never lost the war and I'm living proof of that fact.

America (USA) Is In A Rebirth, Did The Divine Play A Role

Booker T believed that blacks should strive to be self-sufficient, whereas Du Bois believed that blacks should focus on the best education to be successful and accepted by the larger society. So, here we are today many decades later with most black leadership and black elites having abandoned, deserted, and living as for away from a black community as they can afford.

Except for Funeral homes, old churches and maybe a few barber shops and beauty parlors just about every other black elite business has hauled ass out of black communities. The problem is before one can have a free and independent mentality one first must want to strive to be self-sufficient at all cost.

I believe Blacks today are still following the Du Bois formula of wanting to be loved and accepted by others to prove ones worth. A self-sufficient people don't have a need to prove their worth. They already have respect for themselves and know how to show respect for other people, too.

What kind of a people will vote 90 percent plus for one political party for 50 years and still be on their knees hat in hand. I'm just one lonely neurotic writer with my own opinion; thank God I can still share it without disappearing in the middle of the night.

There are no Juke joints and chitlin circuits anymore. There are no thriving exciting black enterprise zones anymore. In my young days there were many clubs, lounges, and places to go including places for teens to dance and have fun, too. But, back then teens knew how to behave, which they don't today and is the reason very few will provide teen centers anymore.

America (USA) Is In A Rebirth, Did The Divine Play A Role

I remember so well when I was a teenager they had a soda shop in my hometown where teens could hangout and dance. Back then a little bit of money would buy a lot. You could get a foot long slaw dog for 25 cent plus a penny tax. A many of time I would get me a slaw dog and be good to go and just hangout and enjoy myself.

However, with our liberal induced welfare state black culture has almost totally been destroyed. Sad, sad, but be aware the destruction of the black culture is like the canary in the mine.
SIRMANS LOG: 10 JULY 2016, 1532 HOURS.

THE MASS KILLING OF SLAVE BLOOD YOUNG BLACK MALES
Let me say up front I would never be a lawman; it's not for me. Also, I should never be writing an article on this subject because I may step on too many toes. But, knowing me I will proceed. First, I believe an economic collapse or rebirth will soon happen in the USA and all of western civilization. The USA and Western Europe and their welfare state's all are too deep and lost in mass liberalism swamps, period.

In the USA what started our whole culture and financial destruction and decline was the enacting of the 1938 minimum wage law. Enacting that law allowed the liberals to grab and hold power by inflating the dollar, which started our welfare state. Without a minimum wage law the dollar cannot be inflated, period. That said, now lets get down to why so many slave blood young blacks are being killed.

The two main reasons are a lack of respect for

America (USA) Is In A Rebirth, Did The Divine Play A Role

authority and very little self-restraint due mainly to no strong male disciplinarian in the home. However, there are several other lesser factors at play. One of the biggest lesser factors at play is young black males are stereotyped as being aggressive and violent. And that in itself causes a certain amount fear in a lot of people.

Stereotyping is unfair and not a good thing but there is always some truth in every stereotype. Plus, there is also a racial element involved, a white victim can ask why, and all kinds of questions and get away with it whereas blacks seldom can in my view. One can be as docile as a lamb, still occasionally a cop may be abusive but that is the rare exception in my view.

Almost all cops will show restraint if one doesn't show rebellion and aggression. Here is some common sense rules if stopped by law enforcement: Keep both hands on the top of the steering wheel, if told to get on the ground you get on the ground, and above all don't make any fast or sudden moves especially in this day and time. Remember, this is an extremely dangerous time for anyone that wares a badge, and we must have order and some one have to enforce it.

I'm going to do a little ranting:
I believe the biggest failure in the black communities is black leaders and elites. They could establish high pecking order zones near black communities instead of getting as far as they can afford from an all or nearly all black neighborhood. I believe the elites are running away from themselves by deserting and not truly loving and accepting a black identity, just thinking out loud y'all.

America (USA) Is In A Rebirth, Did The Divine Play A Role

I think so called black leadership ought to be trying to get more jobs and promoting positive values themselves in black communities instead of expecting the government and the white man to do all of the providing. Respect begets respect.

THE RAW POWER OF THE USA LIBERAL NEWS MEDIA NOISE MACHINE
There is an old saying that "Beauty is in the eyes of the beholder". Well, our liberal news media noise machine see racism and negativity hiding behind every tree. Positive successful well-meaning people never dwell on the negative; they address the negative and move on. Only shallow small-minded haters dwell on the negative.

I believe our negative liberal news media noise machine is the biggest anti-survival monster in our USA welfare state liberalism swamp. Only repealing our God forsaken insane arch-evil 1938 socialist minimum wage law has the power to drain this swamp.

I believe the November 2016 election only determines our speed toward total doom; only repealing above said law will rein in liberalism's death march toward total doom. Of course 98 percent of the USA population think I'm a fool, nut case, idiot, and don't know what the hell I'm talking about because they can't see what I can see with my great almost supernatural wisdom.

I can't convince anyone of anything, I'm just trying to do God will and fulfill my destiny, glory be to God.
SIRMANS LOG: 05 JULY 2016, 1349 HOURS.

America (USA) Is In A Rebirth, Did The Divine Play A Role

A MUSLIM WORLD FACT BY A GREAT WRITER
I have said it before and will say it again. In my view the biggest problem in the Muslim world is western influence and meddling. Modern western liberalism has all but totally destroyed their traditional strongman system that kept peace for centuries.

The west is determined to make its weak morally challenged welfare state democracies one size fits all replace what has worked for fifteen centuries; it is totally insane in my view, period.
SIRMANS LOG: 03 JULY 2016, 1018 HOURS.

NO SENSE OF HUMOR:
Mexican plane above, it's getting ready to attack, that's dry humor for Christ sake! Screw you if you can't take a joke is my view. Too many liberals have a problem with separating the real from the unreal. Humor is the spice of life, don't be a sourpuss. Hell, you can barely get a comedian to perform on a collage campus anymore because of liberalism and extreme political correctness.
SIRMANS LOG: 01 JULY 2016, 0841 HOURS.

ABORTION ON DEMAND IS STUPID AND MADNESS.
Procreation and future USA human survival is now under siege. Abortion on demand is flat-out murder and pain in the womb in my view. If no one protects the unborn while we have mass gay marriages, the morning after pill, porn galore, and contraceptives to no end, then where will future human being come from?

Without the repeal of our God forsaken arch-evil

America (USA) Is In A Rebirth, Did The Divine Play A Role

1938 socialist minimum wage law there is no future USA survival in my view. The USA is far too deep and lost in our liberalism swamp and only repealing the insane God forsaken arch-evil 1938 socialist minimum wage law will drain this swamp, period. England seems to be finding it way out of their liberalism swamp.
SIRMANS LOG: 28 JUNE 2016, 1043 HOURS.

I WILL NEVER JOIN A BANDWAGON AND PUNK-OUT TO LIBERALISM
Like a broken record, play it again Sam. No minimum wage laws no immigration problems. It doesn't get any simpler than that. No getting rid of minimum wage laws soon no western civilization.

I will go as far as to say the come about of minimum wage laws is the single most cause for the decline and destruction of western civilization, period.

Everybody is thinking that the worst problems for the USA and Western Europe are immigration and finance. However, I beg the difference, I think the gravest problem for the west is culture. Too few teach the young proper norms and traditions due to our welfare states. Also, I think we are now entering an era where my books and writing may become respected.

USA 1938 socialist minimum wage law must be repealed soon or we face total civil disorder and doom, period. The law must be respected. We are a nation that is supposed to be ruled by law not by emotions and sensationalism.

To most liberals at heart gun control means taking all guns out of the hands of law abiding citizens as

America (USA) Is In A Rebirth, Did The Divine Play A Role

their final goal. They plan to do it small baloney slice by slice until it is finally achieved.

My word may not be worth much, but personally I would rather see a candidate lose fighting for the survival of my country than to join a bandwagon and punk-out to liberalism sure doom. Duh, we'll see.

The fatal mistake the last three republican presidential losers made was trying to be an appeaser to everyone and being all over the map. It takes a pit bull like bite down on two or three great issues and never letting up. Otherwise, the all powerful negative liberal news media soap opera like noise machine will drown out any hope of getting any positive message through.

All of this liberal news media talk of being helpful to any republican is disingenuous at best, they want you to lose, lose, and lose.
SIRMANS LOG: 20 JUNE 2016, 2038 HOURS.

I'M SEEING PARTISAN ATTACK DOG LIBERAL PROPAGANDA PARADING AS NEWS, WHEN WILL THE REAL NEWS PEOPLE CARE ABOUT THEIR PROFESSION. IT IS ALREADY ALONG WITH USE CAR SALESMEN.

INSTEAD OF PEOPLE ON TV TRYING TO OBJECTIVELY REPORT THE NEWS AS IS, FAR TOO MANY ARE MAKING, SHAPING, AND DISTORTING THE NEWS TO FIT THERE OWN SUBJECTIVE LIBERAL AGENDA.

HYSTERIA AND MUCK RAKING RULES THE DAY, USA FREE PRESS HAS BEEN TAKEN OVER BY EXTREME LIBERALISM, USA, USA, USA...

America (USA) Is In A Rebirth, Did The Divine Play A Role

IS THE DEMOCRATIC PARTY AND LIBERAL NEWS MEDIA ONE AND THE SAME?
I got news for any republican or conservative that thinks another candidate would fare better with the liberal news media, then you are deluding yourself. I believe the liberal news media and the Democratic Party is one and the same, period.

No one is perfect, but at least "The Donald" is going to fight them "No holds barred tooth and nails win lose or draw". The liberal news media steam rolled over the last three republican presidential losers without even having to break a sweat, but not so with Mr. Trump, he is going to take it to the mat.

As a writer of great wisdom one thing I have learned is persistence and determination alone are omnipotent, and I think most super achievers knows this.

Due to our welfare state far too many dependent minded people confuses almost any demand for self-responsibility and self-accountability as racism.
SIRMANS LOG: 15 JUNE 2016, 1003 HOURS.

CAN THE USA SURVIVE ITS INSANITY?
I, as a writer of almost supernatural wisdom can only present the big picture on this whole insane horrific violence matter. I believe what is allowing all of this insane unreasonable violence the USA and western civilization is facing today is the result of weak societal discipline.

The primary head of this monster is the welfare state that results from economic minimum wage

America (USA) Is In A Rebirth, Did The Divine Play A Role

laws that blocks built-in free market place societal discipline. The subheads from this monster is out of control liberalism, the destruction of our nuclear and extended family system, the failure to teach and enforce proper norms and traditions to our young, etc.

We now face an out of control political correction liberalism swamp with moten-gators and every kind of anti-survival monster known to man. All seems to be lost, but there is a savior on a white horse standing ready to ride in and save our way of life by draining this swamp.

One simple act will start the healing process that will save our nation and way of life. That act is to repeal the God forsaken insane arch-evil 1938 socialist minimum wage law. Otherwise, there is no hope; the USA will continue to deteriorate until our phony joke of a free market place economy totally collapses.
SIRMANS LOG: 13 JUNE 2016, 1102 HOURS.

WRITER BELIEVES TRUMP REPRESENTS THE GREATEST THREAT TO OUT OF CONTROL LIBERALISM SINCE THE "NEW DEAL".
I'm going to say something maybe I shouldn't. I believe the dread and fear of Trump by the Dem's and liberals are so strong that some epic high level back stabbing by the Dem's won't surprise me. I believe the writing is on the wall and all of the liberalism marbles is at stake, here.

I believe the Democratic Party and the liberal press is one and the same and on a mission of one thing, political destroy "The Donald" at all cost. I personally believe that anyone failing to vote against the USA Supreme Court being taken over

America (USA) Is In A Rebirth, Did The Divine Play A Role

by liberalism is either a liberal or a fool or both. Duh. There goes our right to bear arms.

It is impossible to have a genuine true free market place economy with a minimum wage law in place. The key to the whole USA problem is: Ronald Wilson Reagan said it years ago, "Government cannot solve our problems government is the problem".

Repeal the poison pill 1938 minimum wage law then a true free market place will kick in and save our freedom and keep millions from starving when this world economy soon collapses. Otherwise, we can kiss the USA goodbye as a free and independent nation, we don't even make a lot of our own military equipment anymore.
SIRMANS LOG: 08 JUNE 2016, 1106 HOUR

45TH PRESIDENT OF THE UNITED STATES OF AMERICA: DONALD J TRUMP?
I've said it before and will say it again, Trump forces one to make an emotional choice, "Love him or leave him". His core followers have chosen to love him and after that he can't do no wrong. The ones that have chosen to leave him goes the full range from tuning him out to outright hate.

In private life when one chooses to leave someone they can't stand, usually "Out of sight out of mind" means it is over and done with. However, with Trump running for president and being on TV so much, "Out of sight out of mind" is not so easily done with. The emotional turbulence one wanted to leave behind is now forced to deal with it coming at them from the TV.

America (USA) Is In A Rebirth, Did The Divine Play A Role

I'm one that believes that emotions affect everyone in some way; it seems to get in the air. To evoke strong emotions I believe is a gift that Trump has, and the effect can't be understood using reasoning. Sure, Trump has the ability evoke strong emotions, but the issues that he is addressing are what truly woo his core supporters.

What now really seems to be coming into focus is Trump actually just might win this whole thing, but it won't be due to just his supporters. If Trump wins it will be because it boils down to two choices. The first choice is the democrats paired with liberalism and the second choice is the republicans paired with conservatism.

Personally I don't believe Trump can accomplish most of what he promises, but if he can save the Supreme Court from a liberal takeover, he got my vote. And I believe that most reasonable men/women of common sense and sound judgment will come to that same conclusion. I believe continuing down this road of liberalism we are on leaves no chance of the USA surviving, nil.

At least with Trump out of control liberalism will be put in check and the Supreme Court saved. Yet, the fact remains after years as a welfare state now most Americans can't recognize a survival threat, physical or moral even if it slapped them upside the head.

I'm no genius or rocket scientist, but I know if liberals get total control of the Supreme Court the second amendment and our right to bear arms is history. After many, many years our welfare state has produced an out of proportion amount of naive shallow minded liberals that can't see past their noses.

America (USA) Is In A Rebirth, Did The Divine Play A Role

I'm not a liberal or conservative I'm a realist. And I assure you there is a 100 percent fact that USA citizens will lose their right to bear arms if liberals take over the Supreme Court, period. After our guns are gone it will be only a matter of time before we lose individual freedom followed by private property rights, period. Liberals can't see this coming but I can my friend.
SIRMANS LOG: 25 MAY 2016, 2259 HOURS.

NEW ADD ON UPDATE CONCERNING USA PRESS: 05 JUNE 2016, 1417 HOURS.
The thing about liberals and those that are shallow and uninformed is usually some form of pain is the only thing that forces them to see the light and become enlighten. The downside is we all are in the same survival boat and when all of our freedom and private property rights are gone, oops, now liberals finally see the light. Duh.

Individual freedom is the rare exception in history and it can't exist very long unless there is a genuine true free market place economy to maintain discipline. Otherwise, creeping do-good liberalism at some point will force a demand for some form of authoritarian rule just to maintain order and some sanity; the USA is nearing that point.

However, there is one last chance to save the USA and western civilization, the USA must repeal our arch-evil 1938 socialist minimum wage law, period. A minimum wage law blocks the disciplinary power of a free market place economy and allows liberalism to grow unabated out of control.

And another thing: I believe for the most part

America (USA) Is In A Rebirth, Did The Divine Play A Role

today's free press is about as useless as tits on a boar hog. Most are shallow and liberal and in many cases distorts the news instead of objectively reporting it.

In no way am I criticizing all members of the USA free press, I still think there must be a free press for freedom to exist.
SIRMANS LOG: 05 JUNE 2016, 1743 HOURS.

PS: Haters and those that are against you will try to make you a liar and perfectionist to dehumanize you. I never fall for it, people don't love you because you are perfect, people love you for being human and not perfect.

GREAT WRITER SHEDS A TEAR
(READ ABOUT JOBS GOING OVER SEAS JUST BELOW)

Knowing that my country cannot survive unless our strong nuclear and extended family system is restored is why I plod on. I know that 95 percent or more of the people who read my views vehemently disagrees and feel that I am mean and uncaring.

Sure, I'm neurotic and no saint, but no one has to tell me how it feels to be beaten down, ridiculed, humiliated, laughed at, rejected, and told that I would never amount to anything. I have experienced it all and more. I almost never speak personally about myself because I feel it is self-serving, so forgive that brief relapse, I carry on.

I learned fairly young that except in rare cases people self-destructs and blames it on others. I learned that if one can genuine love and forgive it

America (USA) Is In A Rebirth, Did The Divine Play A Role

is almost impossible for anyone to mentally destroy you. As a rule you will almost never find those that can genuine love and forgive in mental wards, in prisons, and loser on the streets or else where.

Nothing has advanced civilization more than determine individuals with an idea or conviction, and against all odds stayed the course, like this writer, Freddie L Sirmans Sr.
SIRMANS LOG: 24 MAY 2016, 1223 HOURS.

Blaming other nations for our jobs being driven over seas or out of the USA is one the biggest lies that has ever been told. No problem has ever been solved by blaming others for ones own weakness or lack of discipline. The problem with the USA and has been for a long time is out of control government spending, period. No government can support a welfare state very long, time's up.

Every business must make a profit or go out of business. And the cold hard fact is the USA economy would have collapsed back in the early 1990's unless a way was found to cut expenses, that way was a mad dash to find the cheapest labor.

The cheapest labor couldn't be found here in the USA because able-bodied men were already getting a SSI check or sponging off a mother, daughter, or some other female family member.

I'm age 73 now but when I was a kid my grandmother got a check and I still think that was the greatest thing to ever happen to the elderly. However, a welfare state destroys the nuclear and extended family system and there never has and never will be a society that survives with that being

America (USA) Is In A Rebirth, Did The Divine Play A Role

the case, period.

All "Wealth" and I mean with practically no exceptions comes from some form of private business profit and the truth is USA businesses don't produce enough profit to support our welfare state. So, how in the hell can you bring jobs back if a business can't afford all of the local, state, and federal taxes, plus license fees, permits, and countless other government mandates.

Businesses trying to make a profit to survive are why the jobs were driven over seas in the first place. Love me or hate me I am only trying to give you the cold hard reality facts. The only thing that has a chance of bringing jobs back and saving the USA and western civilization is to repeal our insane arch-evil 1938 socialist minimum wage law. And you can take that to the bank.

Socialism: I'm hearing just south of us down in Venezuela with their experiment in socialism and the ignoring of profit has them eating family pets and standing in line all day for food. I believe if the Dem's keep power and liberalism prevails that is where the USA will be in just a few years.

I believe unless the insane Arch-evil 1938 socialist minimum wage law is somehow repealed the USA cannot remain a free nation. Right now most liberals hate profit and don't think it matters. There is no way to keep order and remain a free people with that prevailing mentality, our mostly liberal free press has failed to educate and keep the people truly informed.

Boo! I'm your boogieman.
SIRMANS LOG: 18 MAY 2016, 2343 HOURS.

America (USA) Is In A Rebirth, Did The Divine Play A Role

WRITER, FREDDIE L SIRMANS, SR. PREDICTS TRUMP WILL PICK A WOMAN RUNNING MATE
I think there is a 90 percent possibility that Trump will choose a woman running mate due to his ease of comfort working with strong women in his past. I constant hear of Trump placing strong women in top position throughout his company.

No one knows including him until he makes the final decision, but the percentage of him picking a woman is almost overwhelming.
SIRMANS LOG: 17 MAY 2016, 1114 HOURS.

Any conservative that believes our welfare state beast will allow social programs to be cut with pain and them remain in power is a fool in my view. If republican and conservatives do get a Trifecta in November 2016 they will have one last chance to save the USA and western civilization.

Plus, they can save the USA and western civilization and keep power at the same time by repealing the Godforsaken insane arch-evil 1938 socialism minimum wage law. Doing that will untie our all powerful free market place economy which will absorb all blame and save the USA and western civilization.

That is the only hope of saving individual freedom in the world today, otherwise liberalism will prevail. Liberalism is going to drive the USA into a dictatorship or some other form of authoritarian rule, period. It is impossible to retain a free society without discipline, responsibility, and accountability, which is fast going by the wayside here in the USA.

America (USA) Is In A Rebirth, Did The Divine Play A Role

I am a great writer folks, I believe it but when has anyone ever taken my advice, never.
SIRMANS LOG: 15 MAY 2016, 1630 HOURS.

I think most of you have heard the saying "Being dead right", so who wants that? I think when it come to politics many of today's conservatives are just plain shallow and lacks a true understanding of human nature, period.

Sure, for a conservative to focus on cutting social programs is sensible and the right thing to do thirty years or more ago, but today in 2016 it is just plain shallow, dumb, stupid, and a recipe for getting booted out of power. And it is a waste of time because our welfare state beast will never allow any worthwhile cuts anyway.

This full-blown super welfare state we have today has far too many government dependents for any individual or political party to put a dent in it and remain in power. Sure, this welfare state tolerate conservatives now because conservatives holds the moral high ground, but at the first sign of any real hardship and pain due to social programs cuts all conservatives will be booted I assure you.

This great country was built on conservative values and today's conservatives are right for wanting to do the sensible thing and live within our means, but they are too shallow to realize that our welfare state beast is much too powerful. I repeat it is shallow, dumb, and stupid to think any individual or political party can force responsibility and accountability peacefully on our full blown welfare state beast, it Ain't gonna happen.

America (USA) Is In A Rebirth, Did The Divine Play A Role

This is where my almost supernatural wisdom comes into play and I will explain. When speaking of force almost everyone will think in terms of physical force, which is out of the question. The reason a genuine true free market place economy is so successful and will produce far more production than any other system known to man is because of its discipline.

Discipline is the same key ingredient found in every successful system. Nature itself operates on its own law of free "Natural selection". All great nations fall from within and nothing on earth is capable of taking down our welfare state beast, except a true genuine free market place economy, period. Our USA today no longer even comes close to having a true free market place economy.

If conservatives expect to save our USA they have one chance and one shot before being booted out of power, otherwise it is political suicide to expect to take down our welfare state beast and survive in power.

The only way to save the USA and western civilization is to untie the USA economy by repealing the 1938 minimum wage law then a true free market economy will kick in and save our civilization, nothing else has the power to save us. Repealing the 1938 minimum wage law will drain the liberal swamp, boom the economy, and then new growth will abound unhindered, otherwise we will just continue on our path to sure doom.
SIRMANS LOG: 12 MAY 2016, 1749 HOURS.

SELF-RIGHTEOUSNESS GONE AMUCK
Priorities, priorities, priorities, we here in the USA are fast on our way of not having a country, yet

America (USA) Is In A Rebirth, Did The Divine Play A Role

some in high places has their priorities upside down. My great beloved homeland is being ripped to threads by liberalism and ignorance, but without a doubt my first priority is to do what I can to help rein in liberalism.

I may be on the losing side and never get to taste the reward of high achievement, but in defeat my soul will rest knowing I never gave comfort to out-of-control liberalism. Liberalism in itself is not a bad thing; in fact liberalism can be a good thing and make the world a far safer and better place for us all.

However, like food, sex, or anything out-of control, out-of-control liberalism is going to kill us, period. Repealing the insane arch-evil 1938 socialist minimum wage law will re-balance and bring liberalism back under control that is the only thing that can possibly save the USA and western civilization.
SIRMANS LOG: 09 MAY 2016, 1633 HOURS.

**BEGGARS CAN'T BE CHOOSY
NO TRUE CONSERVATIVE WILL CUT OFF HIS NOSE TO SPITE HIS FACE OR CUT THE BABY IN HALF, GOOD RIDDANCE.**

REMEMBER, IT IS THE COUNTRY A TRUE CONSERVATIVE LOVE AND WANT TO SAVE, NOT EGOS, AND CERTAINLY NOT ABOUT HELPING PUT FIVE LIBERALS ON THE SUPREME COURT. DUH?

When you are $20,000,000,000,000 in debt as far as I'm concern you are a beggar like it or not. Let me say up front voting for Mr. Trump was not my first choice but I feel I would be a fool not to in the

America (USA) Is In A Rebirth, Did The Divine Play A Role

future. I would never help put five liberals on the Supreme Court. However, I'm a writer folks and I write what I truly believe.

Before our welfare state and insane arch-evil 1938 socialist minimum wage law the USA could talk tough and really back it up. Back then the citizens was independent and almost no one was dependent on the government for hardly anything. Now, lets fast forward to the year of 2016, we are a full blown top heavy welfare state with millions upon millions solely dependent on government for survival.

Admit it or not the USA is totally interdependent and need others to survive as much as they need us. In fact all of these liberal induced government dependents have to be fed there is no stable traditional nuclear and extended family safety umbrella to fall back under, the welfare state has destroyed that.

Even if no one else has the wisdom to see it, I know the only thing that can save the USA and western civilization is to ban all minimum wage laws. That is the only thing that can rein in liberalism and save us. Banning all minimum wages laws will restore the inner fabric of our nation and wean the overwhelming masses off of the government titty.

The days of the welfare state is over because all wealth comes from some form of private business profit and liberalism is destroying that more and more every day. What the USA have now is a wobbly kneed top-heavy p.... of an economy that is here today but could be gone tomorrow. Yet, liberalism is hammering the final nails in our coffin while my wisdom is totally ignored. Lord have

America (USA) Is In A Rebirth, Did The Divine Play A Role

mercy.
SIRMANS LOG: 05 MAY 2016, 1740 HOURS

NEW ENTRY: 01 MAY 2016, 1403 HOURS.
Saving the USA and western civilization is simple; just ban all minimum wags laws. Minimum wage laws fuels inflation and inflation fuels welfare states all to the detriment of long term human survival.

The USA and western civilization can't be saved until the old tried and true norms and traditions are first restored, and no amount of money and good jobs alone will do that. Unless all minimum wages laws are banned to rein in liberalism nothing can save the USA.

If your culture and morals are almost totally corrupted more wealth only acts as an enabler to create bigger problems.
SIRMANS LOG: 01 MAY 2016, 1439 HOURS.

Sometimes it seems like I'm the only one with the wisdom to see that the minimum wage law is what gives government almost total power over the private sector. Before the insane arch-evil 1938 socialist minimum wage law was enacted each individual business decided what wages and prices to operate on and unrestricted competition purged out all inflation.

The minimum wage law is what gave the liberals the power to create our welfare state beast back in 1938 by inflating our currency to no end. And ever since that day our culture, morals, and almost everything else has gone to hell in a hand basket.
SIRMANS LOG: 29 APRIL 2016, 1234HOURS.

America (USA) Is In A Rebirth, Did The Divine Play A Role

All great civilizations falls from within, here in the USA I see it coming every day. The problem with the fallacy of masses of people jumping on a wishful thinking bandwagon is it's like expecting a pot of gold at the end of a rainbow.

The thing about a welfare state is it destroys discipline to the point that very few has a clue as to what raw bare boned survive is all about, I'm seen as a nut case but in survival terms nothing could be further from the truth.

There never has and never will be a nation or society that survived without a stable nuclear and extended family system, period. I hate to say this and hope I'm wrong on this, but I feel western civilization with it's welfare states no longer has the societal discipline, raw wisdom, or the will to survive a full scale economic collapse.

Only banning all minimum wage laws can force the necessary societal discipline on us to prevent our total self-destruction. Liberals and liberalism with its creation of our welfare state is what got us in this dire fix. Its insane to think a liberal parading in conservatives clothing will save us, it ain't gonna happen, yet snake oil is being bought right now on a mass scale.

First things first, nothing can save the USA unless we get back to the basics and reestablish a strong nuclear and extended family system again, banning all minimum wage laws will do just that.

Today most people has forgotten or don't know the basic foundation and building blocks necessary for human society to survive long term, I will give you a brief crude walk through. The number one

America (USA) Is In A Rebirth, Did The Divine Play A Role

foundation building block is the nuclear and extended family system and ours are in almost total ruins.

Another foundation building block is to safeguard our small farmers and home gardeners for emergency backup bartering capacity in case our economy collapses, if the economy collapsed today almost no one would have anything to eat or to barter with. And above all the welfare state has blocked strong males from passing on proper norms, traditions, and morals that in the past safeguarded future generations.

Only by banning all minimum wage laws can the necessary societal discipline be forced upon us to save us from ourselves. I am a lone writer with no connections or source of inside information.

In private I'm sure the liberal news media and the Dem's are gloating and patting themselves on the back. Sure, they tolerate Mr. Trump now because they are so convinced that he will lose to Mrs. Clinton.

However, once the general election begins the liberal news media will show no mercy in trying to destroy this great honorable businessman that truly means well. They will leave no stone unturned looking for muck of every kind. You mark my word. Will they fail, no one knows, we'll see? SIRMANS LOG: 26 APRIL 2016, 2323 HOURS.

America (USA) Is In A Rebirth, Did The Divine Play A Role

SECTION #2: A great little fable I wrote many years ago.

Chapter 1

Once upon a time there was a little town called Health-land kingdom, located right off the big super MD highway leading to the great cure-all metropolis. In this town lived vitamins, minerals, herbs, humans, and other nutrients.

The town's main goal was to keep all of its citizens healthy because anyone that they failed to keep healthy would have to face terrible traffic jams on the super MD highway leading to the great cure-all metropolis.

Jim-Niacin (vitamin B-3). Jim-Niacin doesn't stand alone; he is a member of the very powerful B vitamin family. In Health-land Jim-Niacin's job is essential to promote life and good health. He regulates the metabolism and assists in other body processes, even though he is needed in small amounts compared to proteins and carbohydrates.

As a coenzyme Jim-Niacin works to make sure the human body functions as it should. There are two major types of vitamins: the water soluble and the oil soluble.

America (USA) Is In A Rebirth, Did The Divine Play A Role

Jim-Niacin belongs to the water-soluble type vitamins, therefore his doses must be replaced everyday because the human body doesn't store his doses like the oil soluble type.

Since Jim-Niacin is only one member of the very powerful B vitamin family he shouldn't work alone; he should be balanced with other B vitamin members. Jim-Niacin is not a bad or evil fellow, but he does have a bad reputation.

Humans are afraid of Jim-Niacin and rightly so because in too high doses he may damage the liver, or in too low doses he does no good. But, that is not the only reason human fear Jim-Niacin. Jim-Niacin deals with circulation and the skin, and he will heat the skin up like it is on fire and turn it as red as a beet.
When this happens to a human for the first time, it will scare some humans half to death, but don't be put off, the flushing of the skin is normal when dealing with Jim-Niacin. It's not pretty or pleasant but that is how Jim-Niacin unclogs the capillaries and small blood vessels throughout the body.

Captain Fredrico (human). Orry Fredrico is one of many humans that Was born and raised in Health-land Kingdom. Orry Fredrico is a Carpenter by trade, but as long as he

America (USA) Is In A Rebirth, Did The Divine Play A Role

Could remember he loved the sea. As a small child he would stand by The ocean for hours just staring out to Sea.
As a teenager he would try to Hop aboard any boat going salt water Fishing. During his senior year in high School he went on one of those deep Sea fishing cruises that goes out for Four or five hours at a time. On this Cruises he met Jan Flemmings. Jan Also loved the sea and they instantly Became attracted to each other. Within days Jim started dating Jan.

VC (vitamin C). VC also belongs To the water-soluble type of vitamin. VC is truly a heavyweight among Vitamins. VC is known as a very Power antioxidant. He is a mighty Human body protector. He protects the human body against harmful effects of pollution. He helps to prevent cancer. He helps to lower cholesterol and other protection functions.

Scurvy is a disease that moves in when there is a deficiency in vitamin C protection. Years ago, passengers on ships on long voyages without fresh fruits and vegetables had a problem dealing with scurvy.

Jan Flemmings (human). Jan is a Health-land Kingdom toy

America (USA) Is In A Rebirth, Did The Divine Play A Role

soldier's brat. Just like Captain Fredrico she has always loved the sea. She was mostly unanchored until she met her soul mate Orry Fredrico. At first she thought he loved the sea too much and would not be a good provider, but his dreamy bedroom eyes soon won her over.

VE (vitamin E). VE belongs to the oil soluble type of vitamin. VE is another mighty antioxidant. VE is very important in fighting cancer and cardiovascular disease. Vitamin E is a giant in so many ways. VE is a natural blood thinner. He promotes good blood circulation, he promotes healthy skin, healthy hair, and so many other healthy body functions. Vitamin E actually belongs to a family of eight but falls into two major groups. These two groups are tocopherols and tocotrienols. It is the alpha-tocopherols form that is the most potent. That is the group VE belongs to.

John-Pyridoxine (vitamin B-6). John-Pyridoxine like his cousin Jim-Niacin is a member of the very powerful B vitamin family. The fact is John-Pyridoxine is involved in more bodily functions than any other single nutrient. John-Pyridoxine deals with both the mental and physical health.

America (USA) Is In A Rebirth, Did The Divine Play A Role

He deals with water retention, sodium and potassium balance, and fights hard against allergies, arthritis, asthma, carpal tunnel syndrome, and on and on. Just like his cousin Jim-Niacin, John-Pyridoxine shouldn't fight alone; he should be balanced with other members of the mighty B vitamin family.

Mister Disease. Mister and his family showed up one day in Health-land Kingdom. No one seems to know where he came from. All anyone knows is he is mean and evil. He has no friends and is known to attack humans sometimes without provocation.

He has no conscience and will attack anyone that is weak and helpless. The town and kingdom has tried to keep him out, but somehow he always sneaks back in. Our vitamins, minerals, herbs and others nutrient citizens have done a good job fighting him off, but Mister Disease is a very, very tough customer.

Jim-Niacin and the other nutrient protectors of Health-land Kingdom were joyfully patting themselves on the back because they were doing a good job protecting the city's population from Mister Disease and

America (USA) Is In A Rebirth, Did The Divine Play A Role

his cohorts. Jim-Niacin decided to telephone his cousin John-Pyridoxine. Jim could hear the phone making its fourth ring.

"Hello," said John-Pyridoxine.
" This is Jim-Niacin, I decided to give you a call and touch base on a matter that I've been tossing around in my mind lately."
"Tell me about it," said John-Pyridoxine.

"Well, I've been thinking that all of the vitamins, minerals, humans, herbs, and other nutrient citizens should get together and have a big town hall meeting. What do you think."

"I think it is a very good idea," said john-Pyridoxine.
" Good, then it's a go, I'm going to start right away making plans," said Jim-Niacin. "John you take care now, I'll talk to you later."
" Bye," said John-Pyridoxine.

Chapter 2

    Orry Fredrico and Jan Flemmings got married after a one year engagement. Orry got an associate degree in carpentry from the local technical college. Twenty five years later Orry and Jan are now the parents of a seventeen-year-old son Rob, and a fifteen-year-old

America (USA) Is In A Rebirth, Did The Divine Play A Role

daughter Melinda.

Almost everyone calls Orry by his nickname Captain Fredrico after he bought his first boat about fifteen years ago. The boat was a fourteen footer with a big Mercury motor. Captain Fredrico now operates his own contracting business.

It is almost six o'clock p.m. when Captain Fredrico lets himself in the carport door which opens directly into the kitchen. He found his wife Jan bending over checking her meat loaf in the oven.

"Hello dear," said Captain Fredrico in a somewhat tired voice.
" Hello Orry, how did your day
" Pretty good, but my right wrist that's been bothering me the last couple of weeks seems to be getting worse, especially at night after I fall asleep. Sometimes I wake up with a numb tingling in my right hand. It feels like somebody is sticking pins in my hands."

"Orry, I think you need to check with one of the vitamin citizens. That sounds like something John-pyridoxine might be able to help you with."

"I think you are right dear, I will give him a call in a few days.

America (USA) Is In A Rebirth, Did The Divine Play A Role

After Marrying Orry, Jan Fredrico decided to postpone a career of her own. Becoming a full time housewife and mother was very fulfilling to Jan. She even took on the awesome job of home schooling her kids.

VC (vitamin c) enjoys his job in Health-land Kingdom taking care of its citizens. He has a very good reputation. Humans were using him probably more than any other vitamin. Being one of the most powerful antioxidants, he was in great demand these days.

In fact, he was being used to fortify many of today's foods. He thought the town hall meeting was a great idea. Why didn't he think of it? The vitamins and other nutrients were doing a good job fighting off Mister Disease, but he knew that they couldn't let their guards down, ever.

Just like VC, VE (vitamin E) is another very powerful antioxidant but of the oil soluble type. VE is probably in even greater demand these days than VC. With so many humans becoming diabetics these days, VE with his natural blood thinning power is a real workhorse. VE is also looking forward to the big town hall meeting coming up soon.

America (USA) Is In A Rebirth, Did The Divine Play A Role

On this Monday morning John-Pyridoxine was kicking back at his office when the phone ring.
" Hello," said John-Pyridoxine.
" May I speak to John-Pyridoxine?" said the voice on the line.

"This is he," said John-Pyridoxine.
" I'm Captain Fredrico and I've been told you may be able to help me concerning an ailment. I believe I have a case of carpal tunnel syndrome."

"You have the right vitamin, that is one of my many areas of expertise."
" Then you will be able to help me," said Captain Fredrico.

"Hold on a minute, I didn't say that. Let me explain the situation here, then I can tell you what I may be able to do. Listen Captain, I'm going to explain what I do, and it should take care of your problem, but then it may not. If I can't cure it, then I recommend you take the super MD highway to the cure all metropolis."

"I understand," said Captain Fredrico.
" Now, first off," said John-Pyridoxine, "my maximum dose is 300 mg. per day, that way I will not damage any nerves. In most cases

America (USA) Is In A Rebirth, Did The Divine Play A Role

100 mg. of my dose will cure the problem. The golden rule with taking any nutrients is don't take more than the recommended dose, because too much of anything may cause damage, and never take nutrients on an empty stomach. So, Captain if you understood everything I said, come by as soon as possible. We have a walk in policy."

"Thank you sir, I should be there within the hour."

      Mister Disease is very upset with himself for being unable to do more damage in Health-land Kingdom. He feels he should be able to bring in more of his friends like cancer, AIDS, and even some of his very old friends like the black plague.

He was getting fed up with those damn vitamins, minerals, herbs, and other nutrients. The thing about those nutrients is they are keeping him from getting a foothold in Health-land Kingdom. He feels that if he could just get a foothold he would be able to start an epidemic.

Mister Disease decided that he would just have to work harder. Sooner or later those humans are going to think that they are safe and slack up on utilizing the nutrients. That is the time he plans to throw his best punch. He feels that if his friend

America (USA) Is In A Rebirth, Did The Divine Play A Role

AIDS just keeps up the pressure, he has the best shot at causing an epidemic.

Most humans don't know Jim-Niacin and many of those that do tend to fear and avoid him. As one of the smallest members of the powerful B vitamin family, being unknown is about to change. The reason is Jim-Niacin along with his cousin John-Pyridoxine are the ones that called for and organized the town hall meeting coming up in a few weeks. The whole thing was originally Jim-Niacin's idea.

Since then Jim has invited the town fathers and secured all of the permits needed to stage such an event. Jim has contacted other town nutrients and humans, many of them had never heard of him, or knew who he was.

Chapter 3

Captain Fredrico had lived in Health-land Kingdom all of his life and he loved this town. Captain Fredrico got an invitation from Jim-Niacin to attend the town hall meeting coming up in a few weeks.

Captain Fredrico had heard the name Jim-Niacin before and even

America (USA) Is In A Rebirth, Did The Divine Play A Role

knew he was a member of the mighty B vitamin family, but that was about all he knew about Jim-Niacin. He didn't know what kind of work or anything else Jim-Niacin did.

Captain Fredrico had heard that the vitamins and other nutrients citizens had become concerned about the health of Health-land Kingdom. The main work our nutrient citizens do is protect our human population from characters like Mister Disease and his friends.

The nutrients knew that cancer and AIDS had almost destroyed a few other towns in the Kingdom. The town hall meeting got Captain Fredrico to thinking. The mayoral election will be coming up in about a year. Captain Fredrico decided that he was going to throw his hat in the ring. Of course he would have to talk it over with his wife Jan first.

After putting in a hard day's work, on his drive home Captain Fredrico thought about the pesky dry skin that had been plaguing him for years. It has slowly become more and more of a problem as time past.

Now it has become a real nuisance. It has come to the point that he has to lotion down almost his whole body every time he takes a shower. He feels that is unmanly, only women like to lotion their bodies. He has tried everything, but to no avail.

America (USA) Is In A Rebirth, Did The Divine Play A Role

He had even got on the crowded super MD highway and went to the cure all metropolis, but still to no avail. At the cure all metropolis all they did was to prescribe an extremely expensive body cream that did little better than over the counter creams.

He felt truly at his wits end. There didn't seem to be any hope, he would just have to accept his miserable fate. As Captain Fredrico let himself in the carport door, Jan was making a salad.
" Hello, dear," said the Captain in a husky sexy voice.

"Hello, sweetheart," said Jan in a wooing voice as she dropped everything and rushed over and planted a seductive kiss on her husband's left cheek.

"Now, you go ahead and clean up, dinner will be ready in a few minutes. By the way Rob complained about a bout of indigestion after lunch."

"Did you check with Mr. Blue Page?" said the Captain.
" Yes, he gave me the names of several nutrients that work in that area. The two nutrients that I decided to use were Stewart-Ginger Root and Henry-Acidolphilus. Each one of them gave me heavy doses to give Rob as needed."

America (USA) Is In A Rebirth, Did The Divine Play A Role

"Good, now let me go ahead and wash up, then you can tell me all about it later." After the Captain and all of the family had sat down to dinner and the blessing was said, the Captain revisited the subject of Rob's indigestion.

"How is your stomach feeling now, Rob," said the Captain.
" It's fine now, dad, since Mom had a couple of the nutrients treat it."
" I wasn't sure what to do until after my talk with Mr. Blue Page," said Jan.

"Mr. Blue Page gave me the names of several nutrients that work in the area of indigestion. These are the names that Mr. Blue Page gave me that deal with indigestion: Stewart-Ginger Root, Calvin-Fenugreek, Bonnie-Papaya, Henry-Acidophilus, and Sammy-Oat bran tablets.

He also stressed that they did their work with either tablets or capsules."

"Excuse me for changing the subject, I have a very important announcement to make," said the captain.

"Jan, the mayoral election is coming up in about a year and I would like to know if you have any objections to me throwing my hat into

America (USA) Is In A Rebirth, Did The Divine Play A Role

the ring."

"Gee, I don't know? I've never thought about being a politician's wife. Do you think you can win?"
"Dad, I love it, I think it is a great idea," said Melinda.
"Me too," said Rob.

"I can't guarantee you I will win, but I believe if I get out there and shake enough hands I'll have a very good shot."
" Dad, I'll campaign for you," said Melinda.

"Honey, If you really want to run, then count me in as your number one supporter," said Jan.
"Then it's all settled You are looking at the next mayor of Health-land Kingdom."

Ever since John-Pyridoxine had agreed to help his cousin Jim-Niacin organize the big town hall meeting coming up soon, he had stayed busy calling and talking to the citizens of Health-land Kingdom.

Chapter 4

Mr. Disease was aware of the big town hall meeting coming up in a few days, and he definitely was not pleased about what he was hearing. The word was they were going to try to get rid of him. Mr. Disease was not going to let that deter him, that

America (USA) Is In A Rebirth, Did The Divine Play A Role

had been tried before with his ancestors all throughout history.

Sure, the discovery of DDT, penicillin, and modern antibiotics had given his family some big setbacks, but some of his old friends like tuberculosis were beginning to make a comeback, and the new kid on the block, AIDS, was really beginning to raise hell.

Mr. Disease felt that as far as he was concerned, let them have all of the town hall meetings they want to, it was not going to put him out of business.

Mr. Disease watches the super MD highway often and as far as he could tell it was becoming even more crowded each day. Even at the big super cure all metropolis they haven't been able to get rid of his best friend Mr. Cancer. Mr. Cancer is still doing an awful lot of damage.

On this Monday morning Jan Fredrico   sure didn't want to battle the traffic jams on the super MD highway going to the cure all metropolis. It was just one of those days, Her daughter was down with a cold and she herself was dealing with a slight kidney infection.

She didn't know? Maybe it was something she ate that was causing

America (USA) Is In A Rebirth, Did The Divine Play A Role

her back a slight ache in the area of her kidney. She knew that it would save her a lot of money and time if she called Mr. Blue Page and found out which vitamins, minerals, herbs, or other nutrients that specialized in the areas of their ailments.

Jan decided to give the nutrients twenty-four hours to do their work, then if there was no obvious improvement she would get on the crowded super MD highway to the cure all metropolis. Jan dialed Mr. Blue Page. The voice on the line said, " You have reached Mr. Blue Page directory."
"Mr. Blue Page, this is Jan Fredrico. My daughter has a cold and my kidneys have a slight ache. I would like for you to give me the names of the nutrients that specialize in the areas of our illness."

"Very well, madam. In the area of the kidneys, the association of VC and Cranberry handle that, and in the area of colds and flu, the association of Garlic, Echinacea, and Golden Seal handle that. Will that be all, madam?"

"Yes sir, and thank you very much," said Jan. Taking advantage of their-walk in policy, Jan didn't have to wait long before she was able to see VC, the very powerful vitamin C antioxidant.

"Mrs. Fredrico," said VC, " We

America (USA) Is In A Rebirth, Did The Divine Play A Role

give our doses in mostly tablet form. I am of the water soluble type, the body does not store my doses. Taking too much of my dose is washed out with the urine. But, taking too much of my dose also may cause diarrhea or stomach soreness in some humans.

Rule number one for dealing with your kidney problem is to keep drinking lots of water, then take 2000 mg. of vitamin C tablets three or four times a day after a meal, also take 2000 mg. of cranberry fruit capsules three of four times a day after a meal. That should take care of your problem, Mrs. Fredrico."

Jan next proceeded to take her daughter by the association of Garlic, Echinacea, and Golden Seal to take care of her cold. After a short wait Jan and her daughter were lead in to see Hannah-Garlic.

Hannah-Garlic came from one of the most powerful and popular of all herb families. Even the Roman army would not go into battle without a member of the garlic family coming along.

Hannah-Garlic instructed Jan to give Melinda throat lozenges if needed, then give her a dose of about 1400 mg. of odor controlled garlic, three or four times a day after a meal, also give her a 1500 mg. dose of combination echinacea-golden seal

America (USA) Is In A Rebirth, Did The Divine Play A Role

three or four times a day after a meal.

"You should see some obvious improvement in twenty four hours; if not take the super MD highway to the cure all metropolis.

"It is also helpful to take heavy doses of vitamin C after a meal at the beginning of a cold. But, only at the beginning of a cold, because if congestion sets in, vitamin C tends to make it worse. Warning: Never take vitamin C or others nutrients on an empty stomach," she said.
After thoroughly going over everything, Hannah-Garlic said, " That is it, Mrs. Fredrico, do you understand all of my instructions?"

"Yes, Herb Garlic and thank you very much." While driving home Jan reminded herself to do her neck exercises when she got home. It has been quite awhile since stress has caused her neck to tense up, but she Decided that she would go ahead and do the exercises anyway.

Jan believed that feeling stress is a normal part of life. The better one learns how to deal with life's frustrations the better one will be able to cope with stress. Stress affects people in many different ways. It may affect some in physical ways such as headaches, neck aches, shoulder aches, etc.

To deal with physical aches it is

America (USA) Is In A Rebirth, Did The Divine Play A Role

helpful to do these exercises. These exercises are done sitting on the side of the bed. Sit on the side of the bed with feet apart flat on the floor for balance. With both hands rolled into a fist, place them thumbs inward down on the bed several inches from the body on each side.

Start the first exercise by twisting the neck and entire upper body counter-clockwise as far as possible, then twist the neck and entire upper body clockwise as far as possible. Do these exercises in sets of one hundred as many times as one desires.

Start the second exercise by leaning the head as far as possible on the right shoulder, then lean the head as far as possible on the left shoulder. Do these exercises in sets of one hundred as many times as one desires.

Start the third exercise by leaning the chin as far as possible down on the chest, then lift the head backward as far as possible. Do these exercises in sets of one hundred as many times as one desires.

Chapter 5

On the morning of the big town hall meeting, Jim-Niacin followed his daily routine of taking care of the

America (USA) Is In A Rebirth, Did The Divine Play A Role

citizens of Health-land Kingdom. Jim-Niacin tried to take care of all loose ends concerning the town hall meeting by making a lot of last minute phone calls. He rehearsed the program with his cousin B-12 who would be the moderator for tonight's town hall meeting.

At seven o'clock p.m. sharp Jim-Niacin arrived at the local high school gymnasium, the location of tonight's town hall meeting. The meeting was scheduled to start at eight o'clock p.m. There were several satellite trucks already in place when he arrived. There were the local radio and TV crews as well as reporters from the big super cure all metropolis.

Arriving at the high school was familiar territory for Captain Fredrico. He had walked at the high school track three or more times a week for several years. The high school track was a popular walking place for the citizens of Health-land Kingdom. Captain Fredrico felt that walking or some type of physical fitness program is a must to maintain good health.

It is a fact that one in good physical condition has almost a ten times better chance of surviving a heart attack, stroke, or any ailment. Also, physical activity plays a big role in controlling diabetes. A big help with diabetes is controlling what one eats. Most humans can control diabetes by cutting way back on

America (USA) Is In A Rebirth, Did The Divine Play A Role

starches and sweets and taking a chromium picolinate at each meal.

One needs to eat less meat and include more peas, beans, fresh fruits, and raw vegetables. One needs to include at least one raw fruit or vegetable at each meal because cooking and microwaving food destroys all enzymes and most vitamins.

Enzymes are involved in almost every bodily function, especially the digestive process. Enzymes are mostly divided into two groups: digestive enzymes and metabolic enzymes. The digestive enzymes break down food enabling the body to function properly.

The human body manufactures a limited supply of enzymes, but in order to prevent indigestion and other digestive problems one should get as many enzymes as possible from raw food. Otherwise, the body's limited supply becomes depleted.

Jim could see that there was going to be a very big turnout for tonight's event. It seemed like his hard work on getting the word out had paid off. Several tables were set up at one end of the gymnasium to try to accommodate as many as possible on the big panel of vitamins, minerals, humans, herbs, and other nutrients.

Everyone were handed a

America (USA) Is In A Rebirth, Did The Divine Play A Role

program as they filed into the gymnasium. It read that, "We will not be able to accommodate everyone due to the time it would take. The moderator will ask all questions, but he will take a few written questions from the audience." At exactly eight p.m. sharp B-12 (vitamin B-12) strode up to the podium.

"Greetings, my fellow vitamins, minerals, humans, herbs, and other nutrients, I'm B-12 your moderator for tonight's town hall meeting," he said. "First I would like to welcome our town's fathers, celebrities, and all other dignitaries to this town hall meeting. Now, I would like to thank the vitamin that made it all happen. He is truly another unsung hero. Many of you here tonight probably have never heard of him, but all of the while he has been out there everyday doing his job. He is one of the lesser known members of the powerful B vitamin family. I am proud to say this truly unsung hero is my first cousin Jim-Niacin (vitamin B-3). Stand up, Jim."

"Thank you, thank you, thank you," said Jim-Niacin as he stood and the audience loudly applauded. "Now," said B-12, "before we get into questions and answers we are going to let several members on our panel down here give their name and vocation. We will start with me. I'm B-12 (vitamin B-12). One of my many jobs is to assure proper

America (USA) Is In A Rebirth, Did The Divine Play A Role

digestion and the absorption of food."

"I'm Jane-Ginkgo Biloba. I'm a very well known herb. I'm mostly Known for improving memory."
"I'm Sammy-Oat Bran Tablets. I'm known for my fiber. Fiber does so many things, for now I will mention just two, I lower the blood cholesterol and help stabilize blood sugar."

"I'm Eddie-calcium. I'm a mineral and I do many things. I'm most needed for strong bones and teeth and to help lower blood pressure."
"I'm Mary-Magnesium. I'm a mineral and of the many things that I do, enzyme activity is most vital. I also assist calcium and potassium uptake."

"I'm Sue-Chromium. I'm a mineral and of the many things that I do, maintaining stable blood sugar levels is most vital."
"I'm VA (vitamin A). I'm a vitamin and lesser known antioxidant. My main job is protecting the eyes and some skin problems."
"I'm Dee Dee (vitamin D). I'm a vitamin, and I'm needed for the absorption of calcium and phosphorus."

"I'm Ned-Zinc. I'm a mineral and of the many things that I do, keeping the prostate gland healthy is most vital."

"I'm Kenny-Saw Pametto. I'm an

America (USA) Is In A Rebirth, Did The Divine Play A Role

herb, my main job is to prevent the enlargement of the prostate gland."

"I'm Gina-Evening Primrose Oil. I'm an essential fatty acid. I'm a necessity that cannot be made by the human body. I do many things, but improving the skin is my favorite."

"I'm Patty-Potassium. I'm a mineral. Of my many jobs I will name just a few. I help maintain a healthy nervous system and regulate heart rhythm, also I help control the body's water balance."

"I'm Hannah-Garlic. I'm an herb. I detoxify and protect the body against infections. I help lower blood pressure, aid circulation and perform many other functions."

"I'm Henry-Acidophilus. I'm a friendly bacteria. My main job is to aid digestion."

"I'm Bonnie-Papaya. I'm an herb. I aid digestion. I'm good for heartburn, indigestion, and bowel disorders."

"I'm Brad-Cranberry Fruit. I'm an herb. I'm helpful for fighting infections of the urinary track."

"I'm Stewart-Ginger Root. I'm an herb. I do many things, but cleaning the colon, reducing spasms, and stomach cramps is my favorite."

"I'm Calvin-Fenugreek. I'm good

America (USA) Is In A Rebirth, Did The Divine Play A Role

for the stomach, intestines, eyes, asthma, sinus, inflammation, and lung disorders. I also increase sexual desire."

"I'm Edna-Echinacea. I'm an herb. I have anti viral properties and I help boost the immune system. I'm very helpful against colds and flu."
"I'm Gene-Golden Seal. I'm an herb. I act as an antibiotic, and have anti-inflammatory and antibacterial properties."

I'm David-Dandelion root. I am an herb. I help cleanse the blood stream and liver and increase the production of bile. I'm used as a diuretic. I help reduce uric acid and improve functioning of the stomach and other vital organs.

"That is the last introduction we will have time for," said B-12. "Now, I will ask the panel a few written questions given to me from the audience, but first let me explain our role here. Number one is we try to be the first line of defense on protecting Health-land Kingdom from Mr. Disease and his cohorts.

"We have some citizens who don't believe in us and won't use our services. The next thing is we don't try to be everything to everybody, our services and abilities are limited.

We encourage anyone that has doubts or don't believe in us to take the super

America (USA) Is In A Rebirth, Did The Divine Play A Role

MD highway to the cure all metropolis. Still, there is a lot we can do to keep Mr. Disease and his friends from gaining a foothold here in Health-land Kingdom.

"Very important: When taking the super MD highway to the cure all metropolis, make sure you tell them which of our services you are maintaining.

"Now, when I ask a question to the panel, please let those that specialize in that particular area of expertise answer the question. Time will not allow me to ask but only a few questions. My first question to the panel is what can we do to combat prostate disease?" he asked.
"I'm Ned-Zinc, and I recommend 50 mg. of zinc per day."

"I'm Larry-Pumpkin Seed Oil, and I recommend 1000 mg. of pumpkin seed oil per day."
"I'm Kenny-Saw Pametto, and I recommend 160 mg. of saw pametto extract twice per day."
"I'm VE (vitamin E), and I recommend 1000 I.U. of vitamin E per day."
"I'm Jim-Niacin, and I recommend my maintenance dose of 250 mg. of niacin per day."
"Is there anyone else?" said B-12. "So, that gives us five weapons to fight prostate disease, and I'm pretty darn sure that anyone that arms themselves with these weapons

America (USA) Is In A Rebirth, Did The Divine Play A Role

will be able to keep Mr. prostate disease away for a very long time, if not forever. My next question to the panel is what can we do to deal with diabetes disease?"

"I'm Sue-Chromium, and I recommend 200 mg. of chromium picolinate three times a day at meal time. I also would like to elaborate a little on this terrible disease.

"Diet plays a major role in controlling this terrible disease. Everyone with this disease should be able to home check his blood sugar level and keep it under control. But, controlling blood sugar is not the only problem diabetics face.

"There are problems with the eyes, blood circulation, and many others. There is a problem with nerve damage (neuropathy) especially in the lower extremities," she concluded.

"I'm VE (vitamin E), and I recommend 1000 I.U. of vitamin E per day. Being a natural blood thinner makes me a great asset to a diabetic."

"I'm Jim-Niacin, and I recommend my maintenance dose of 250 mg. of niacin once per day for one not showing any diabetic symptoms. On the other hand, for anyone experiencing the symptoms of diabetes, especially numbness in the lower extremities I recommend my

America (USA) Is In A Rebirth, Did The Divine Play A Role

unclogging dose of 250 mg. of niacin twice per day.

"Too high of a dose of niacin can cause liver damage and high blood sugar levels, but too low of a dose does no good. The 500 mg. maximum dose per day seems to be just enough to be effective.

"There have been many lower extremities cut off because of diabetes, but I truly believe that if they had only given Jim-Niacin a chance I would have saved some of those limbs."

"Is there anyone else?" said B-12. "There it is folks, three powerful weapons to deal with this scourge diabetes. Now, for the final question of the evening, the question is what can we do to prevent extremely dry skin?"

"I'm Gina-Evening Primrose Oil, I'm an essential fatty acid and I'm one of the good oils that the body needs for beautiful skin. I recommend 1000-3000 mg. of evening primrose oil per day."

"I'm Jim-Niacin. In my view problems with dry skin, toe nail funguses, dandruff, and other skin problems is almost always a problem with blood circulation especially in the capillaries and small blood vessels.

"For extremely dry skin I

America (USA) Is In A Rebirth, Did The Divine Play A Role

recommend my unclogging dose of 250 mg. twice per day after a meal until the extremely dry skin condition has been cured, then throttle down to 250 mg. once a day for maintenance. But, be aware, most humans fear me, and for good reason, because my doses are no Sunday picnic or stroll through the park. My doses may heat up your skin like it is on fire and turn it as red as a beet.

"This flushing process is unpredictable, sometimes it will not happen at all, then other times it will last anywhere from five minutes to thirty minutes. It may not be pleasant, but it is my only way of unclogging the capillaries and small blood vessels," said Jim-Niacin.

"Is there anyone else?" said B-12. "What more could one ask for; those were two of the most powerful remedies that I ever heard of in dealing with a pesky humiliating dry skin condition.

"Remember, a dry skin problem is not something to be taken lightly, because you can see what is happening to the outer skin, but what's taking place inside with the vital organs could be a lot worse.
"Citizens of Health-land Kingdom, that will end our town hall meeting for tonight, I would like to thank everyone for coming. Have a safe drive home," he said.

America (USA) Is In A Rebirth, Did The Divine Play A Role

Chapter 6

Captain Fredrico was very impressed with the town hall meeting, especially learning how to deal with his long time dry skin problem and toe nail fungus. It had got to the point that he hated to take a shower.

It was bad enough struggling through the warmer months of the year, but the approach of winter was almost terrifying because a dry skin problem becomes much worse during the winter months. Much of the time during the winter he had to resort to what is called a bird bath by washing only his arm pits and private area. He had tried all kinds of oils, both internal and external. He had traveled on the super MD highway to the cure all metropolis, but all to no avail. Since the town hall meeting he had started off on Jim-Niacin's unclogging dose of 250 mg. of niacin twice a day after a meal.

The resulting benefits were obvious within a couple of days. Within days the treatment was so effective that the captain could barely wait to jump into the shower for the slightest reason. Also, within days his toe nails had started clearing and should be completely clear within a few months.

Also, in a few months the mayoral election will be taking place.

America (USA) Is In A Rebirth, Did The Divine Play A Role

Captain Fredrico felt very good about his chances of winning. According to the latest poll he had a four point lead.

That night as he and Jan were setting in the den watching TV, Captain Fredrico said, "You know, Jan, if I do become mayor of Healthland Kingdom I'm going to recognize Jim-Niacin by declaring a Jim-Niacin day."

"I know, dear, how much you love Jim-Niacin. He made it possible for you to be able to take regular showers again without you having to lotion down almost your whole body."
"I don't care how much he is feared and misunderstood," said the Captain. "As far as I'm concerned Jim-Niacin is a miracle vitamin."

"I agree, my darling husband, about Jim-Niacin's abilities, if humans would just give him a chance he would save most of the lower extremities that are being lost because of Mr. Diabetes Disease."

The Captain got up from his recliner, walked over to Jan and gave her a warm tender kiss on her waiting luscious lips and said, "I'm off to bed, dear, I'll wait up for you."
"I won't be long, dear," said Jan.

Things had been rather calm in

America (USA) Is In A Rebirth, Did The Divine Play A Role

Health-land Kingdom for the last few months VC, VE, and John-pyridoxine all were very busy taking care of the town's population. About the only thing going on was the mayoral election coming up very soon.

They all thought the town hall meeting did a lot of good for the community. They felt it educated the citizens that there was a lot they could do for themselves concerning their health care.

That means that one will not have to jump on the super MD highway for the slightest little pin prick or minor inconvenience. Sure, there is only so much we vitamins, minerals, herbs, etc. can do to promote health, we don't try to be everything to everybody.
After the town hall meeting Mr.

Disease was steaming mad. He was even thinking of calling a meeting of all the different diseases. The nerve
of those vitamins, minerals, humans, herbs and other nutrients trying to get together and put him and his friends out of business.

They want to try to put his most successful friends like cancer, diabetes, heart disease, and AIDS out of business. He was not having it; that was not going to be tolerated. Mr. Disease started planning.

America (USA) Is In A Rebirth, Did The Divine Play A Role

He would try to attack their left flank by bringing back some of his old friends like the Black Plague, Tuberculosis, and West Nile, next he would try to rush their right flank with AIDS to try to split their force, then he would try to rout them up the middle with lots of Cancer and Heart Disease.

I will take no prisoners. Who do they think this is, this is Mr. Disease and I don't play, I even quit school because they had recess. It is on. How dare they have this town hall meeting to try and get rid of me and my friends.

After a long hot summer the day of the mayoral election had finally arrived and it looked like it was going to be a big turn out. At seven o'clock p.m. Captain Fredrico, Jan, Bob, and Melinda had comfortable seats at election headquarters. All of the election precincts closed at seven o'clock p.m. sharp.

The captain and his family started watching the tally on the big electronic board as the precincts came in. Captain Fredrico jumped out to an early four point lead and was able to maintain the lead throughout the night as the precincts came in. Then, finally the election supervisor announced, "Citizens of

America (USA) Is In A Rebirth, Did The Divine Play A Role

Health-land Kingdom the mayor elect is Orry Fredrico." Within seconds several microphones were thrust in Captain Fredrico's face.

A reporter was almost yelling, "Captain Fredrico, how does it feel being the mayor elect of Health-land Kingdom."

"First, I would like to thank my family and all of the volunteers that worked so hard on my behalf to make this happen. Next, I would like to thank all of the citizens of Health-land Kingdom who had the faith and trust in me and backed it up by turning out to vote for me.

"Also, I would like to inform those that did not vote for me that I will be mayor of all the citizens of Health-land Kingdom. Finally, I would like to thank my opponent for a good clean hard fought campaign. Thanks again everyone. Good night."

Chapter 7

About one month after Captain Fredrico had been sworn in as mayor of Health-land Kingdom, he announced that the first Saturday in March would be recognized by the town as Jim-Niacin's day.

On the morning of the first Saturday in March Mayor Fredrico

America (USA) Is In A Rebirth, Did The Divine Play A Role

stood at the podium at Healthy living park before a very large crowd.

"Citizens of Health-land Kingdom, today as your mayor I am proclaiming today as Jim-Niacin's day. We have on hand plenty of free food, drinks, and entertainment. To kick off this festive day, I'm going to deliver this short speech about the vitamin citizen we are celebrating today.

"Citizens of Health-land, Jim-Niacin is sort of an enigma. Many here had never heard of him, and of those that had, many of them fear and hate him. Still there is a great many that love this vitamin to death.

"I myself am one of those that dearly love Jim-Niacin and the good work he does. I am not telling you what I heard about Jim-Niacin, I'm telling you what I've personally experienced with my dealing with Jim-Niacin. I'm giving it to you first hand, straight from the horse's mouth.

"As I've told my wife and many others, I don't care what anyone says, to me Jim-Niacin is a miracle vitamin. This small, quiet, lowly member of the powerful B vitamin family is a Godsend as far as I'm concerned. As a proud virile human male I think of the many, many years that I suffered with extremely dry skin.

America (USA) Is In A Rebirth, Did The Divine Play A Role

"For years I tried everything to get relief from this annoying dry skin condition. Even at the cure all metropolis they just prescribed an extremely expensive body cream that did little better than cheap over-the-counter lotions.

"Bathing and warm water had become the enemy. Washing only arm pits and the private area was becoming the norm, and I just hated my predicament. To me cleanliness is next to Godliness.

"Sure, I had heard of Jim-Niacin, but it was mainly bad stuff, I never knew about his real power until I attended the town hall meeting. Over the years the dry skin problem was getting worse. Some type of fungus had invaded my toe nails and my skin was losing its luster in a few locations.

"The battle for healthy skin was a battle I knew I was losing , but no one could help me and I didn't know what to do. All of my life I've never been a quitter, I knew there was an answer, the problem was finding it, so I just kept on searching and searching.

"I was at my wits end, nothing or no one seemed able to help me find relief from my extremely dry skin condition. Then, at the final hour when all seemed lost and there was no hope left, Jim-Niacin came riding in on a big white horse at the town

America (USA) Is In A Rebirth, Did The Divine Play A Role

hall meeting.

"At the town hall meeting Jim-Niacin gave out his unclogging dose of 250 mg. twice a day after a meal. The first thing is I must warn you that taking Jim-Niacin's unclogging dose is no cake walk or stroll through the park. That is the reason many who have tried taking Jim's doses don't like him and is afraid of him.

"When Jim goes to work unclogging those capillaries and small blood vessels it is not pleasant by any means. This flushing process varies in intensity, sometimes it may be mild, then at other times your skin may feel like it is literally on fire.

"This flushing process may last anywhere from five to thirty minutes, but seldom lasts more than thirty minutes. I have no evidence to support this, but I believe diabetes itself is caused by a deficiency in niacin, chromium, and a few other nutrients.

"Citizens of Health-land I could go on and on praising Jim-Niacin because in the past he truly has been an unsung hero. I will add this and come to a close. Don't ever go over his maximum 500 mg. daily dose or it could cause liver damage.

"In closing, I will assure you that his unclogging dose got rid of my dandruff, dry skin, toe nail fungus,

America (USA) Is In A Rebirth, Did The Divine Play A Role

etc. Stand up Jim-Niacin and say a few words," concluded Captain Fredrico.

As Jim-Niacin arrived at the podium he stood tall and proud. The audience went wild with applause, then chanted, "We love you Jim, we love you Jim, we love you "Thank you, thank you, thank you," said Jim-Niacin, "and may God bless this great town and keep it healthy always."

THE END

FREDDIE L SIRMANS SR.
WEBSITE: FLSirmans.com

www.ingramcontent.com/pod-product-compliance
Lightning Source LLC
Chambersburg PA
CBHW070105210526
45170CB00013B/749